HOW TO BALANCE YOUR BUSY LIFE …
GOD'S WAY

~~

Traci L. Warren

xulon PRESS

Dedication

This dedication is to my husband, Dodie, the love of my life and to Jake and Shelby
my precious children. Thank you for allowing God to use you in growing me for His
glory. Thank you to my mom and dad for their love, support, and prayers over the years.
Appreciation is given to my extended family and to the Titus women in my life for helping
me grow up in the way I should go, so that when I became older I did not depart from it.
Special thanks goes to Billie, Evie, Shelli, Emily, Karen, and Melanie for your countless
hours and godly counsel. Also, to the ladies at Birchwood and the pastors that gave me
advice: Thank you all for encouraging and loving me through this process.
Each of you holds a special place in my heart.

Table of Contents

Introduction

Welcome to *How to Balance Your Busy Life … God's Way!* I am so glad you have chosen this Bible study to help you get a handle on balancing your life.

It is no coincidence that you were led to this Bible study. You see, I have been praying for you. I asked the Lord to draw every woman He knew who needed balance and organizational skills in their lives. He chose you.

This Bible study is a six-week in-depth study. It is also a six-week commitment to God and to your Bible study classmates. Each day you will journey through God's holy Word to find the answers for how to get your priorities in order and how to live a balanced life. This Bible study was written with busy women in mind; each lesson should only take 20 to 30 minutes, allowing time for prayer and praise! Day one through day five will end with the same two questions.

Question #1 – "What did the Lord teach me through His Word today?" Simply jot down what you learn each day from the Bible. Personalize your answers as if you are speaking to God Himself.

Question #2 – "What have I done today that has eternal value?" Each day we do many things that have eternal value, in being a loving wife, mother, friend or neighbor, setting a godly example, praying, reading our Bible, or sharing our faith in Jesus. We are called to store up our treasures in Heaven. The point of this question is to understand what is important to God, not to be boastful about what "I" have done for Him but what "He" is doing through me each day. Reflect on the activities of your day and write down one or two things that God is doing through you. This question has been important in my life because it has challenged me to focus more on my first priority … God!

Each week consists of four daily lessons and a Summary for each week, plus a few Tips and Ideas. Day five will be a review for the week and the topic of discussion for your next class. Each lesson should be completed before your class time.

Discussion Questions: You will have Discussion Questions from time to time during your Bible study. These are the questions you will discuss during your class time.

All Bible references have been obtained from the New International Version (NIV) unless otherwise noted. Also, you may notice that pronoun written in reference to God is capitalized. (Example: He, His, Him, etc.) This is done in reverence and respect for our Father.

At the end of this Bible study you will find a few charts: "Balance Chart," "Chore Chart," and a "Bible Study Prayer Log." You have my permission to copy as many charts as you need to successfully achieve personal balance in your life.

But first, let me ask you this question. Who is Jesus to you? Is He your Father and best friend? Is He your Savior?

John 3:16 says, "For God so loved the world that He gave His one and only Son, that whoever believes in Him shall not perish but have eternal life."

Romans 3:23 – "For all have sinned and fall short of the glory of God."

Romans 6:23 – "For the wages of sin is death, but the gift of God is eternal life in Christ Jesus our Lord."

Romans 10:9 – "That if you confess with your mouth, "Jesus is Lord," and believe in your heart that God raised Him from the dead, you will be saved."

You cannot begin to live a life of balance if Jesus is not in the center of it.

Do you know without a shadow of a doubt that you are going to heaven when you die? It says in **John 3:3**, "I tell you the truth, no one can see the kingdom of God unless he is born again." If you do not remember the exact moment that you asked Jesus to come into your life, then it is entirely possible that you have not received salvation. You cannot enter heaven without it.

Jesus Christ loves you so much that He died on the cross for you. If you will ask Him, He will cover your sins and see them no more.

Please pray right now: "Jesus, I believe you are the Son of God, and that you died for me to forgive me of my sins. I believe that You were raised from the dead on the third day and ascended into heaven. Please forgive me of my sins and come into my life. Lord, I ask You to save me and make me a new person."

Praise God! This is the most important decision you have ever made in your life. Now you have the assurance that you will go to heaven when you die! Be sure to tell your pastor or a Christian friend of your new decision so they can help you in your new walk.

2 Timothy 3:16-17 - "All Scripture is God-breathed and is useful for teaching, rebuking, correcting and training in righteousness, so that the man of God may be thoroughly equipped for every good work."

As we search the Scriptures in the weeks ahead, let us be equipped for every good work.

Week One – Balancing Act

Day One – Setting Godly Priorities

Day Two – Learn How to Say NO

Day Three –Part 1 - God's Top Ten
**   Part 2 - The Lord's Day**

Day Four – Time — A Precious Gift from God

Day Five – Week One Review

Does your life feel like a tornado spinning out of control? Do you wish you could calm the winds of your life and see God sweep away the storm with His mighty hand, replacing it with a bright and beautiful day?

What are God's priorities for my life? Am I so busy because I don't know when to say no? What priorities are God's top ten? How does God view the way I spend my time? What are my priorities anyway?

Do you wish you had the answers to these questions? Are you ready to start living a life that is in balance with our Creator? Well, my friend, you are about to begin a new way of living. Let God show you through His holy Word what His priorities are and how He wants you to spend your time. Open your hearts and minds. Let Him teach you something new each day.

WEEK ONE MEMORY SCRIPTURE

"But seek first the kingdom of God and His righteousness and all these things shall be added to you" (Matthew 6:33 NKJV).

DAY ONE

Setting Godly Priorities

This week we are going to focus on our personal journey to God's glorious kingdom. We are so caught up in the here and now of our daily lives that we don't think much about why we are here or what value this time on earth will merit in eternity.

What are you doing with the time God has entrusted to you? Are you traveling through life's journey with a purpose?

Paul wrote a letter to the people of Colosse because he had heard that they were holy and faithful.

Colossians 1:9-14: "For this reason, since the day we heard about you, we have not stopped praying for you and asking God to fill you with the knowledge of His will through all spiritual wisdom and understanding. And we pray this in order that you may live a life worthy of the Lord and may please Him in every way: bearing fruit in every good work, growing in the knowledge of God, being strengthened with all power according to His glorious might so that you may have great endurance and patience and joyfully giving thanks to the Father, who has qualified you to share in the inheritance of the saints in the kingdom of light. For He has rescued us from the dominion of darkness and brought us into the kingdom of the Son He loves, in whom we have redemption, the forgiveness of sins."

May this be our prayer as we journey through this time on earth, that we would have the knowledge of His will through all spiritual wisdom and understanding, and that we would live a life worthy of the Lord, pleasing Him with every good work!

Sister, He has rescued us and redeemed us. He has qualified _____ (fill in your name) to share in the inheritance of the saints in the kingdom of light with the Son He loves. WOW! It can't get any better than that! What good news to remember after a long hard day — that the King of the Universe in His glorious splendor wants to share His inheritance with us!

Please read Matthew 6:33.

What are we to seek first?

_____

Now read Mark 12:30.

List four ways we are to love the Lord.

_____
_____

When setting godly priorities, we need to seek first the kingdom of God and love Him with all of our heart, soul, mind, and strength.

The questions for today may seem a bit self-oriented, but it is important that you answer them honestly. We will review Day One as we near the end of our study.

What are your priorities? Please list them in order.

1. _____   4._____
2. _____   5._____
3. _____   6._____

Are they in order? How much time do you spend weekly on each priority that you listed? Go back to the list above and write down the estimated time you actually spend on each priority. Some of us work a 40-hour workweek outside of the home, and some of us are raising young children or may be home schooling. Be honest with yourself. You cannot say that God is your first priority if you only spend two hours a week with Him. However, it is quite possible to place God as your first priority in whatever you do if you are living your life for Christ. Are you going through each day praying in all situations, reading your Bible daily, praising Him and sharing Christ with others? Or, do you begin your day in a rush, overwhelmed by your daily activities and never giving God a single thought? Believe me, this was a lesson I had to learn. It was so prideful of me to say that God was my first priority when I didn't include Him in my day.

Don't worry if you feel your priorities are out of whack! This is only Day One of Week One of this Bible study! As you start reading the Scriptures and giving this issue to God in prayer, He will help you to get them in order. If God has already blessed you with proper balance in this area of your life, then that is cause for giving praise and thanks to Him!

Let me give you an example of my personal priority list in a typical week from a time period in my life in the past.

<u>Past</u> – At this particular time in my life I was going to school and studying a lot. I would typically spend an hour with Jake and Shelby before they went to school each morning and

an hour after school. I would spend about five hours with them on Saturdays and Sundays. I studied eight hours every day for a big test, put in a couple loads of laundry a day, ran a few errands. I cooked the quickest thing I could find for dinner. I said good morning and good night to my husband and gave him a kiss each day! I prayed, "Lord, please let everything go well today, and please help me to retain all that I study." I tucked the kids into bed and said a bedtime prayer. I went to church two hours on Sunday morning and two hours on Sunday night, and I listened to praise music in the car and showered each day!

Let's see what this looks like on a priority list based on the time I spent on each task:

1. School — 56 hours a week
2. Home – (dinner, laundry, housework) 25 hours/week
3. My children — 24 ½ hours a week (how sad)

4. God — maybe 11 hours a week
5. Myself — 10 hours a week
6. My husband? (Well ... poor man!)

I realize that the total hours do not add up to a complete week, but you get the idea.

The following is an example of my personal priority list in a typical week after learning how to balance my life.

Present – Spend around one hour first thing in the morning in prayer, Bible study and praise. Try to help my husband get off to work, spend time in the morning with both of my children with either prayer, a Bible verse for the day, or both. Tidy up around the house, do a load of laundry, then work outside the home for 5 ½ hours a day. Check in with my husband to see how his day is going. Prepare and cook a balanced dinner on most days, have a family sit-down meal, and pray together. My husband and I will spend time with our children and help them if they have questions on their homework. We also spend time together as a couple, going on dates, attending couples Sunday school class, and going to church services on Sundays. I serve on the youth staff, attend Bible studies and during all of this, pray without ceasing!

Knowing the amount of time that I spend on each priority now, my list looks more like this!

1. God
2. My husband
3. My children

4. Work
5. Home
6. Myself

No, I'm not perfect! Most certainly, I'm as human as they come! Not every day goes as planned. If you are a wife or mother, or just have a busy life, you know as well as I do no one is perfect (except Jesus). The two most important lessons that you can get out of this study are these: to know beyond a shadow of a doubt that we were created to have a loving relationship with God, and that we were created to serve Christ with our lives! If you do these two things, everything else will fall into place.

Read Psalm 37:4.

Fill in the blanks.
"_____ yourself in the Lord and He will give you the _____
of your _____.''

What does He tell us to do first?
_____

Yes, if we <u>delight</u> ourselves in the Lord, <u>then</u> He will give us the desires of our hearts.

Ask yourself these questions:

What are the desires of my heart?
_____

What are my goals in life?
_____
_____
_____

What are my dreams?
_____
_____
_____

Goals are dreams with a deadline. Take a moment to think about your life's goals, both short-term and long-term.

What are my goals this week?
_____
_____
_____

This month?
_____
_____
_____

This year?
_____
_____
_____
_____

What do I want to accomplish in my lifetime?

_____
_____
_____
_____
_____
_____

Discussion Question: How do I want to be remembered?

_____
_____
_____
_____
_____
_____

Am I pleased with the way I live my life?

_____
_____
_____
_____
_____
_____

More importantly, is God pleased with the way I live my life?

Do your priorities line up with God's Word? Are you seeking the Lord and His righteousness **first**? Do you love the Lord with all your strength? Think about that for a minute, loving the Lord with all your strength! Imagine for a moment that you are a weightlifter. You must use all of your strength to lift the heaviest weight that you can. Do you love the Lord like that?

What changes do I need to make in my life?

_____
_____
_____

Our life is a journey, and we all have a final destination. Think about how a ship arrives to its final destination. The captain sets the course and directs the ship's path. The ship doesn't go left or right without the guidance of the captain's hand. On life's journey, we are the vessel and Jesus Christ is our Captain.

Read Proverbs 4:25-27.

What does this scripture teach us?

_____

_____

_____

Prayer: Precious Lord, You are the one Who gives me the desires of my heart. Lead me to set goals and to live life according to Your teachings. Lord, I pray that Your Holy Spirit will convict me right now of areas in my life where I need to move out and let You in.

What is the Lord teaching me through His Word today?

_____

_____

_____

What have I done today that has eternal value?

_____

_____

_____

Review your Memory Scripture for Week One.

DAY TWO

Learn How to Say No

Did you find out a few things about yourself on Day One? Do you have areas that are hindering you from living a balanced life?

If so, what are they?

_____

_____

We have to remember that we only have one life to live. I urge you to seek the Lord for proper balance in your life.

Please read Psalm 119:33-40.

Write verse 35 here.

_____

_____

What does verse 37 say?

_____

_____

Re-read verse 40 and fill in the blanks.

Preserve my _____ in your _____.

Dear child of God, this ought to be our prayer. Please take a moment to pray Psalm 119:33-40 to your Savior.

Are you allowing God to direct your path? Are you turning your heart toward His statutes and not toward selfish gain? Are you turning your eyes away from worthless things to preserve your life according to His Word? Are you preserving your life in His righteousness?

If you answered "yes" to these questions, and I hope you did, then you are ready to learn when to say "No" to the things that are not your priorities and say "yes" to what matters most.

The fact is - we belong to God. This is our one and only chance to get this life right.

Some women have a hard time saying "No" to anything that is asked of them! What they don't realize is that saying **no** to the things that are not a priority in life is the same thing as saying **yes** to what is important to them and their families. Saying "No" at the right times will free up some of your time, making you more available for God.

THERE ARE TIMES IN LIFE TO:

ALWAYS ANSWER YES: In obeying God and doing God's will.
ALWAYS ANSWER NO: When the situation is sinful or will lead to sin.

Let's see if I can clarify this "Yes" and "No" thing with a few examples. The first thing we need to do is evaluate the situation or activity. Second, determine if it is on your priority list. Hopefully by this point you have already prayed about your priorities and know what they are. Third, pray about the situation. Fourth, ask yourself if anyone else can do it; and last, answer the question with a yes or no answer.

1. <u>Situation/Activity</u> – My child's first school play.

<u>Ask yourself these questions and answer</u>:
Is this on my priority list? Yes.
Pray about it? I prayed for my child, but I knew that I was going to his play.
Can someone else do it? Yes, but I'm his mother and I should be there for him.
Will I do this or not? Yes, of course I will, this is a no-brainer for me!

2. <u>Situation/Activity</u> – You are so excited about your out-of-town relatives coming to visit you! They arrive at 11pm tonight. You still have to change the sheets on the bed, vacuum, clean the bathroom, grocery shop, then go to the airport. Your girlfriend calls at the last minute to ask if you can baby-sit because she doesn't want to take her children to the mall.

<u>Ask yourself these questions and answer</u>:
Is this on my priority list? No.
Pray about it? Lord, thank you for the blessing of showing hospitality in my home. My top priority today is my family. You know my heart Lord, and that I wouldn't mind watching my friend's children after my relatives leave town, but please help her to understand that I can't do it today.
Can someone else do it? Yes.
Will I do this or not? No, I cannot do this today.

3. <u>Situation/Activity</u> – Today you plan on cleaning house and catching up on the laundry. Your neighbor calls and is on her way to the emergency room with her oldest child. She wants to know if you can watch her baby while she is gone.

<u>Ask yourself these questions and answer</u>:

Is this on my priority list? Yes, right now helping my neighbor is my priority.

Pray about it? Father, please help me to be a blessing to my neighbor and please be with her and her oldest child. Please give the doctors and nurses wisdom to treat this child.

Can someone else do it? Yes, but she called on me and I need to be there for her.

Will I do this or not? Yes.

Get the idea? Put your priorities in God's hands and pray about the situation or activity. Then you will be able to answer yes or no knowing that you have made the best decision.

You will never learn how to balance your priorities until you place God first in every situation and keep Him at the center of your life.

What is the Lord teaching me through His Word today?

_____

_____

_____

What have I done today that has eternal value?

_____

_____

_____

Please write your Memory Scripture for Week One in the space below.

_____

_____

_____

DAY THREE

Part 1
God's Top Ten

Is God beginning to rearrange your priorities? Are you seeing your priorities in His light? We cannot truly identify our priorities without knowing what God's priorities are. Today as we search God's Word we will find out what is important to Him, our Almighty God.

Please read Romans 3:21-31.

Who falls short of the glory of God? (specifically, read verse 23)

_____

Fill in the blanks (Romans 3:25)

"God presented Him as a _____ of _____, through _____ in His _____."

We have all sinned and have need of a Savior.

Read John 14:26

Who is our Counselor? _____

What will He teach and remind us of?

_____

Please read Matthew 22:36-39.

What is the first and greatest commandment?

_____
_____
_____

What is the second commandment that Jesus is talking about?

_____

_____

_____

God instituted the Ten Commandments in the Mosaic Covenant – the Law given by God to Moses at Mount Sinai for the nation of Israel.

List the Ten Commandments in the space provided below. See how many you can list without looking.

1. _____
2. _____
3. _____
4. _____
5. _____
6. _____
7. _____
8. _____
9. _____
10. _____

Now read Exodus 20:1-17 where the Ten Commandments are recorded in the Bible. How did you do in writing them down first from memory?

_____

_____

Please notice that God used the words "commandments" and not "suggestions."

Go back and fill in the commandments that you had trouble remembering.

Why did God give the Israelites the Ten Commandments?

_____

_____

Which Commandment do you have the most trouble with? Why?

_____

_____

Please stop and pray that God will reveal any weak areas that you may have in your life, and that He will provide His strength for you to overcome in those areas.

The truth of the matter is, if you are obeying the first and greatest commandment by loving the Lord your God with all your heart and with all your soul and with all your mind, then you won't have a problem with commandments one through four. If you are obeying commandment number two by loving your neighbor as yourself, then you won't have a problem with the other six!

DAY THREE

Part 2
The Lord's Day

Ah, Sunday, "The Lord's Day;" a day of rest, a holy day devoted to the Lord.

"Hurry, wake up! My alarm didn't go off; did I even set the alarm? Mom, did you wash my pants? Mom, I can't find my slip! Have you brushed your teeth yet? Honey, can you iron my shirt? No, you cannot wear your costume to church! Let the dog out! Is the coffee ready? Mom, have you seen my shoes? What's for breakfast? Grab a breakfast bar and get in the car." Rush, rush, rush, we make it to the car. "Where is my Bible? Did you get the tithe check?" We have to park at the far end of the parking lot where we make a mad dash to the front door, take a big deep breath, put on the church smile, and stroll in as if we have had the most pleasant morning possible. Sound familiar?

Does it matter to God how we spend the Lord's Day? The answer is yes! We need balance on the Lord's Day. We will begin today's lesson by taking a brief look at seventh day observances in Genesis and Exodus and finish with Jesus' resurrection.

<u>God's Seventh-Day Rest</u>
Please read Genesis 2:2-3. Fill in the blanks starting with verse 3.

"And God blessed the seventh day and made it _____, because on it He rested from all the _____ of creating that He had done."

1. **God rested on the seventh day, not because He was tired, but to indicate the completion of creation. The world was perfect, and God was well satisfied with it.**

2. **God blessed the seventh day; He elevated it above the other days. It was a day set apart for the remembrance of the perfection of God's original six-day creation.**

27

3. Notice, God was the only one who rested; He rested because there was no more work to be done. We don't see Adam and Eve come into the picture until later in chapter 2.

Sabbath Day
Now read Exodus 16:1-30.

What did God do for them?

_____

On a side note - Let's not overlook all the grumbling they did. They were not grumbling at Moses and Aaron; they were grumbling against the Lord.

What did the Lord command in Exodus 16:23?

_____

_____

Exodus 16:23 is where the first mention of the word "Sabbath" can be found in the Bible.

Now read Exodus 20:8-11 and fill in the blank.

"_____ the Sabbath day by keeping it holy."

Read Isaiah 58:13-14.

How were the Israelites to treat the Sabbath day?

_____

_____

According to verse 14, what can be found in the Lord?

_____

_____

Recap:
1. The Sabbath day was on the seventh day of the week; this day was holy and set apart from the rest of the days.
2. When the law came down, the Mosaic Law, this day was not only a day to praise God for His creation, but also a day for penitence. This day was set apart to for them to examine their lives and measure them against God's law.
3. God did not want them to work or cook any food on the Sabbath day; He did not want the busyness of life to distract them from worshipping Him.

The Lord's Day

Our day of worship is on Sunday, "the Lord's Day," the first day of the week. Why do we set aside Sunday as the day we come together as a body to worship?

Please read Matthew 28:1-20 and fill in the blanks from verse 1.

"After the _____, at dawn on the _____ _____ of the week, Mary Magdalene and the other Mary went to look at the tomb."

Now read Luke 24:7. What does it say?

_____

_____

Jesus was buried on a Friday and triumphantly rose from the dead on a Sunday, the first day of the week.

Matthew 28:9: "Suddenly Jesus met them. 'Greetings,' He said. They came to Him, clasped His feet and worshiped Him."

Ladies, this was at dawn on Sunday morning. They came to Him, clasped His feet, and worshiped Him! This was the first Sunday morning worship service.

Read Luke 24:13-27. Pay special attention to verses 25-27.

Did you notice how it describes in verse 27 that Jesus explained the Scriptures to them? This was the first Sunday sermon.

Jesus appears to His disciples on the evening of the first day, as recorded in Luke 24:36-49, where the eleven and others were gathered, and "then He opened their minds so they could understand the Scriptures." He also gave them the Great Commission: "repentance for forgiveness of sins will be preached in His name to all nations, beginning at Jerusalem." He also told them to "stay in the city until you have been clothed with power from on high."

Acts 20:7: "On the first day of the week we came together to break bread."

Recap:
1. **Christ rose from the grave on a Sunday.**
2. **The first worship service and the first morning and evening sermon were on the first day of the week.**
3. **We worship on the first day of the week because of the example set by the early church.**

Now read Hebrews 4:1-11.

In Hebrews 4:9-10 it says, "There remains, then, a Sabbath-rest for the people of God; for anyone who enters God's rest also rests from his own work, just as God did from His."

Fill in the blanks of verse 11,
"Let us, therefore, make every effort to _____ that _____, so that no one will fall by following their example of _____."

On the Lord's Day we are to be focused on worshiping, rejoicing, and praising Him in Christian fellowship, giving honor and thanks to our Savior.

Preparation Day

Preparation day is mentioned several times throughout the Old Testament; this was the day before the Sabbath day. Even though the Old Testament law does not bind us anymore, having a day of preparation is a great idea when you are trying to balance your life. We are all aware that in every week Saturday comes before Sunday. We should make it a habit every Saturday to prepare for Sunday. Cook extra food on Saturday to make it easy for yourself on Sunday. Do your chores, have everyone find their Sunday clothes, get them pressed, find shoes and socks and set them out. Then when Sunday morning comes along, you'll wake up thinking, *ah, it's the Lord's Day!*

Please take some time in prayer to your Lord about the way you and your family spend the Lord's Day.

What can I do differently this Sunday to make the Lord's Day a day of rest?

_____

_____

Discussion Question: What changes do I need to make on Saturday to prepare for the Lord's Day? _____

_____

What is the Lord teaching me through His Word today?

_____

_____

_____

What have I done today that has eternal value?

_____

_____

_____

Use the space provided below to write your Memory Scripture.

_____

_____
_____
_____

DAY FOUR

Time — A Precious Gift from God

Do you know anyone who seems to have all the time in the world? The truth is that they don't; they just manage their time wisely. We all have the same 24 hours in a day and only one life to live. We make our own choices as to how we spend our time. It is how we **manage** our time that makes the difference. Today we will get a glimpse of how we are to use the time that God has given us, and we will learn how to live our day-to-day lives with a kingdom purpose.

Job 9:25: "My days are swifter than a runner, they fly away without a glimpse of joy."

Please read James 4:13-15.

What is your life according to this scripture?

_____

Please read Romans 14:5-12.

What will happen when we all stand before God's judgment seat?

_____

_____

Does it matter to Him how we live?

_____

_____

<u>Season of Time</u>
Now Read Ecclesiastes 3:1-8.

What time or season are you in right now?

_____

_____

What gave you peace as you read the scriptures?

_____

_____

Running Out of Time
If you had six months to live, what would you say to the people you love?

_____

_____

_____

_____

How would you treat the people you love on a daily basis?

_____

_____

I need to tell _____ (fill in their name) about Jesus
before it's too late.

Time to Forgive
Read Psalm 103:12, Psalm 145:8-9, and Matthew 6:14-15.

What does your heavenly Father have to say about forgiveness?

_____

_____

If you do not forgive men their sins, your Father will not forgive your sins. Sister in Christ, pray about this; you may need to write a letter, make a phone call, or visit someone.

Who do I need to forgive?

_____

_____

What do I need forgiveness for?

_____

_____

Wasting Time
Do you waste your time? Think about your relationships and the stressful or aggravating situations you may currently find yourself in.

Today we will spend time on an activity that is a two-step process.

LIFE SITUATION CHART

STEP ONE	STEP TWO

Step One: On the "STEP ONE" side of the "LIFE SITUATION CHART" list the current situations that are stressful, hurtful, or aggravating in your life.
Step Two: We will finish this step at the end of today's lesson.

Please don't waste your time on negativity or gossip. Is that the last thing you want to have on your mind or your lips the moment you meet your Savior?

The reason we hear more negativity in the world is because it takes less effort to be negative. Be positive; see the glass half full! I challenge you to be positive. It takes more effort and you will be a better person for it. As a matter of fact, if you are being negative, you are not allowing God to be God in your life or the lives of others. You are trying to fix everything and everyone. Instead, hand all of it over to Him. He will fix it or fix them. If you gossip, that is a form of judging.

Please read Proverbs 24:29 and Romans 12:14-19.

What does the Bible say about the way we are to treat others?

_____

_____

Now read 2 Timothy 4:14-18.

How did Paul handle revenge?

_____

_____

Read 2 Corinthians 10:3-5.

Do you take captive every thought you have to make it obedient to Christ? Y/N

Explain:

_____

_____

Please read Psalm 15:1-3; 17:3; 141:3; Proverbs 17:4; Ecclesiastes 10:20, and 2 Thessalonians 3:11-13.

In your own words, what does the Bible say about how you act and what comes out of your mouth?

_____

_____

Now read Proverbs 31:26-31.

Fill in the blanks of verse 27.

"She watches over the affairs _____ _____ _____ and does not eat the bread of_____."

This scripture is speaking of a woman (who is also a wife) who has a noble character. Can you see that the noble woman minds her own business and does not waste time on gossip?

Think about this the next time you are grocery shopping and you spot her. Yes, I'm talking about "Miss Busybody!" She "knows" all, "sees" all, and you're about to "hear" it all, standing right there in the middle of aisle six!

Read Matthew 7:1-5, Romans 2:1, and Romans 14:10-13.

What does the Bible say about judgment?

_____

_____

God is almighty and has all power. Let us trust Him. He can do a better job of judging than we can.

Step Two: Go back to the "LIFE SITUATION CHART" and write something positive beside each one that you listed on Step One.

Pray every day for the person or situation that you are dealing with. It is very hard to be upset with someone you are earnestly praying for. Trust God and ask Him for His will to be done. Every time I've had a conflict with someone and have truly given it to God and prayed for them daily, He has answered my prayer even better than I could have imagined. God is so good!

All the things we have done out of our own desire, pride or to impress others will be worthless ... it all will have been wasted time in the eternal scheme of things. David was called a man after God's own heart. Wouldn't you love to get to heaven and be known as a woman after God's own heart?

What is our purpose? To serve Christ with our life! God gives us this time on earth to build and strengthen our character for eternity.

Time to Balance
Now we are going to try to put all the pieces of the balancing puzzle together!

Balance Chart: A Balance Chart is a chart to help you visualize the way you spend your time. We have what I call "life categories;" these are your priorities. You will list your priorities on the top line of the Balance Chart and then fill in the way you spend your time during the day in each of the Life Category columns.

You will see that it's not that difficult. If you spend time in each life category, you will begin to bring balance into your life. We will use the next few Sample Charts to help us identify our priorities. Read all three examples and find the one that is the most like the season of life you are in right now. Fill in the blanks on the Sample Chart you choose.

Sample Balance Chart #1
For a Wife and Mother

Relationship with God	Spouse	Children	Home	Work/Friends	Myself
At 7:00am, spent 30 minutes in Bible study, Prayer and Praise. Listened to Praise music while in car running errands. Read daily devotion with family. Prayed throughout the day.	Had a great conversation about this upcoming week-end. Later in the evening, we had some quiet time together. Read daily devotion with family.	Helped the kids get ready for school. Prayed with them. After school, helped them with homework, then they helped me with dinner. Walked with them while they rode their bikes. At bedtime, we read together our daily devotion.	Picked up clutter before I left for work. and started a load of laundry. Washed dishes. Started another load of laundry after getting home. We all picked up the evening clutter before going to bed.	Had a positive but busy day at work. Invited a new girl to lunch to get to know her better.	Went on a fast walk after dinner while the kids rode their bikes. Took a short but sweet bubble bath before going to bed. Ah... Then read for a little while.

In a typical day for a wife and mother, you can see how the balance all comes together. Some of the things you do during any given day, such as family devotions, will go in three different categories: your relationship with God, your spouse, and your children.

This activity is a review of your day, so you will need to fill in the information at the end of your day.

If Sample Chart #1 fits the current situation of your life, fill in the blanks below.

What are three things I did today that included my relationship with God, my spouse, children, home, work/friends and myself?

_____

_____

_____

_____

_____

_____

_____

_____

_____

_____

Sample Balance Chart #2
If You Live on Your Own with Children

Relationship with God	Home	Children	Spouse	Work/Friends	Myself
At 7:00am, spent 30 minutes in Bible study, Prayer and Praise. Listened to Praise music while in car running errands. Read daily devotion. Prayed throughout the day.	Picked up clutter before I left for work. Washed a load of laundry. Washed dishes. Picked up the evening clutter before going to bed.	Prayed for my children and their families. I called my son and asked him how his job was going. I mailed my grandchild a birthday card today.	Prayed: Lord, I am hurting today, please give me your strength to get through this difficult time in my life. Lord you are my husband right now, I am leaning on you.	Had a positive but busy day at work. Invited a new girl to lunch to get to know her better. Went on a walk with my neighbor.	Went on a walk after dinner with my neighbor. Took a long bubble bath before going to bed. Ah... Then read for a little while.

I have not experienced this path of life, but I have received input from women who have. This is simply an example of a balance chart.

Again, you can see how walking with a friend went into two different categories: your work/ friends and yourself. Praying went into the categories for God, Children and Spouse. You will need to customize your chart to your life.

If "Sample Balance Chart #2" fits your life situation, fill in the blanks below.

What are three things I did today that included my relationship with God, spouse, children, home, work/friends and myself?

_____
_____
_____
_____
_____
_____
_____
_____
_____

Sample Balance Chart #3
If you are Single without Children

Relationship with God	School	Home	Work/Friends	Yourself	Dating/Courting
At 7:00am, spent 30 minutes in Bible study, Prayer and Praise. Listened to Praise music while in car running errands. Read daily devotion with my "guy friend."	*Studied for finals with my study group. One of the students was having a hard time understanding the material. I prayed with her and asked God to help her understand the material and give her wisdom and knowledge. Invited her to my singles ministry group this weekend.*	*Picked up clutter before I left for work. Washed a load of laundry. Washed dishes. Picked up the evening clutter before going to bed.*	*Had a positive but busy day at work. Invited a new girl to lunch to get to know her better.*	*Went on a walk in the park after dinner with my "guy friend." After he went home, I returned to my house and took a long bubble bath before going to bed. Ah... Then read for a little while.*	*Went on a walk in the park after dinner with my "guy friend." We read a daily devotion together.*

If "Sample Balance Chart #3" fits your life situation, fill in the blanks below.

What are three things I did today that included my relationship with God, school, home, work/friends, dating/courting, and myself?

_____

_____

_____

_____

_____

_____

_____

_____

_____

_____

Hopefully you are getting the idea; your goal is to spend time in each life category per day. You can see that some of the things you do can be added to more than one category. Keep track of your balance chart for the next couple of weeks. Pretty soon you will be ending each of your days with a sense of contentment and balance. This will become a new way of living for you and your family.

Now it's your turn! At the end of your day today, write your priorities in order and list the things that you did in your life categories.

Each one of us is responsible for the way we live our life. This is our personal journey to God's glorious kingdom. We will all stand before the throne of Heaven and give an account for the way we lived our lives. Let's live with a purpose!

What is the Lord teaching me through His Word today?

_____

_____

_____

What have I done today that has eternal value?

_____

_____

_____

Write your Memory Scripture for Week One from memory. Be prepared to recite it in class.

_____

_____

_____

WEEK ONE SUMMARY

- "Seek first the kingdom of God and His righteousness."
- Our priorities need to line up with God's Word.
- God gave us the Ten Commandments, not the ten suggestions.
- How we spend our time IS important to God.
- Take captive every thought to make it obedient to Christ.

WEEK ONE - TIPS AND IDEAS

Keep a master family calendar for all doctor appointments, games, practices, homework assignments, trash day, dinner dates, parties, holidays, and so on.

Clean out one closet and one drawer each week of our Bible study and you will have six of them finished by the time the study is over! Get drawer organizers for your junk drawers; place a label where each item belongs so it will find its way back to the proper place each time.

Keep an ongoing list of grocery items needed posted on your refrigerator door.

NOTES

_____
_____
_____
_____
_____
_____
_____
_____
_____
_____
_____
_____
_____
_____

DAY FIVE

Week One Review

You have spent all week learning how to set godly priorities. Please know that I am praying for you to seek proper balance in your life by acknowledging what your priorities are.

Please pray before you begin today's assignment that God will show you what His priorities are.

What has God taught me through His Word this week about setting godly priorities, learning to say no, His commandments, and the way I spend my time?

_____

_____

_____

How can this bring balance to the way I spend my time?

_____

_____

_____

What are my action steps for this week?

_____

_____

_____

What can I share with my class regarding the topics of godly priorities, saying no/yes to others and outside commitments, the Ten Commandments, the Lord's Day, and/or time management?

_____

_____

_____

What is the Lord teaching me through His Word today?

_____

_____

_____

What have I done today that has eternal value?

_____

_____

_____

Review your Memory Scripture and be prepared to recite it in your next class.

Week Two – Jesus Is the Center

Day One - A Relationship with God

Day Two - Setting a Routine

Day Three – Praying

Day Four - Praise to Jesus

Day Five - Week Two Review

Our Father in Heaven longs to have a relationship with His children. This is what we were created for. We need to realize that He must come first.

This week we will learn how to have a relationship with God by making Him a priority through Bible study, prayer, and praise.

Our personal relationship with Jesus is extremely important. You cannot have a balanced life if you do not place Him at the center of it. Pray right now with your Savior before you begin this week's lesson.

Prayer: Father, please be the center of my life. Reveal Yourself to me and help me to view our relationship through Your eyes. I pray that this week will be a turning point in my life as I begin to seek You with all of my heart. Help me each day to set an appointment with You through Bible study, prayer, and praise. In Jesus' name I pray, Amen.

WEEK TWO MEMORY SCRIPTURE

"Love thy Lord your God with all your heart and with all your soul and with all your mind and with all your strength" (Mark 12:30).

DAY ONE

A Relationship with God

"Good morning, Lord," is the first thing that should come to our minds when arising in the morning. When you place God first in your day, everyday, everything else will fall into place. Remember Matthew 6:33? "Seek first the kingdom of God and His righteousness and all these things shall be added to you."

Our relationship with God should begin with respecting and appreciating who He is. We need to stand in awe and recognize that He is almighty God!

Please read Matthew 10:37-39. Fill in the blanks.
Anyone who does not _____ his _____ and _____ me is not worthy of me.

Are you seeking the Lord and His Righteousness on a daily basis?
Circle Yes/No

One summer while visiting my hometown of Deer Park, Texas, I met with my friend Melanie Daigle. We were sharing what the Lord had been doing in our lives. I began to tell her of the Bible study that I was writing on how to balance our lives God's way. After explaining that one of the chapters was on building a relationship with God, she got excited, jumped up and said, "I'll be right back!" She breezed back into the room with a few sheets of paper in her hand! She shared with me that the Lord had been working through her life like never before! She had written a "how to" guide on effective quiet time with God. Neither one of us are professionally trained writers, so you can imagine how excited we were to learn that God had led us simultaneously into writing about Him! Her knowledge from God had changed her life! She said, "Traci, if this information will help other women, please use it!" So I did. We integrated our two writings together, and for the next three days you will see how God used both of us to explain how to have a loving relationship with Him. Don't you just love how God works?

One way to accomplish this on a daily basis is through prayer and Bible time.

Making Time for Daily Prayer and Bible Study

<u>**Melanie:**</u>
Are you like me, in that you love the Lord with all your heart and soul, but you just can't get into a routine of daily prayer and Bible study? What I realized is that when I finally did get into a daily routine, my life changed dramatically! The solution was to eliminate the things from my life that were keeping me from getting closer to God. It is the best thing I have ever done. My reason for sharing this is because God has instructed me in His Word. Hebrews 10:24-25 says, "And let us consider how we may spur one another on toward love and good deeds. Let us not give up meeting together, as some are in the habit of doing, but let us encourage one another, and all the more as you see the day approaching."

Here are the key points to remember:

- Realize that God must come first in your life.
- Make an appointment to meet with Him daily.
- Praying is our conversation with God; we are to pray without ceasing.
- Praise the name of the Lord!

Realize God must come first. Before everything else — including your husband, children and yes, even church activities and responsibilities – God must be first in our lives. Just because you are serving God within the church does not mean you have a close relationship with Him or that you are placing Him first. What God really wants first and foremost is for you to be in prayer and to get to know Him better.

Below are some of the blessings that come from making God a priority in your life.

- You will get to know God better by developing an intimate relationship with Him.
- You will gain knowledge and discernment from God's Word.
- You will experience joy and peace even when you are struggling.
- You can openly share Jesus with others and praise Him with no inhibitions.
- You will be content and satisfied in just knowing your Savior.

<u>**Traci:**</u>
Look at the list below and circle any obstacles that you may have.

TV	**Volunteering**	**Family**
Employment	**Computer**	**Exhaustion**
Telephone	**Laziness**	
Housework	**Shopping**	
Errands	**Exercising**	
Reading	**Friends**	
Sports	**Church**	

List any other obstacles in your life that keep you from spending time with God.

_____

_____

We all know that a person must have some down time. We would go crazy or else completely burn out without it! Really evaluate the way you spend your time and be honest with yourself: does watching TV or playing on the computer have eternal value? I'm not saying these things are wrong, because that is between you and God. What I am saying is that *anything in excess* is a sin! This is not the last time you will hear me say this in this Bible study.

TIME: Think about God's time. God's time has eternal value.

Please read Genesis 1:1. Fill in the blank.
In the beginning_____. What more do you need to know? This is stated very clearly; in the beginning – God!

Now read 2 Chronicles 1:10-11.

What does God want us to ask for?

_____

_____

Read 1Timothy 4:7-8.

What does verse 8 say?

_____

Psalm 119:36-37: "Turn my heart toward your statutes and not toward selfish gain. Turn my eyes away from worthless things; preserve my life according to your word."

We all have a life to live and obstacles to overcome, but your relationship with God Almighty must come first. If you have not spent quality time in prayer and Bible study with God, then you will not have the true wisdom and discernment that comes from Him. Give God a chance. He will honor your devotion to Him. That's what He yearns for. He is so faithful to us, my friend; won't you be faithful to Him?

What is the Lord teaching me through His Word today?

_____

_____

_____

What have I done today that has eternal value?

_____

_____
_____
_____

Please review your Memory Scripture for Week Two.

DAY TWO

Setting a Routine

Traci:

When my daughter Shelby was small, I would help her select her clothes and comb her hair. This was our usual morning routine. But one morning I could hear her in her room, so I called out to her but she did not answer. A few minutes passed without an answer from her, I said, "Shelby, are you up?" There was still no response from her, so by then I was getting a little concerned. A few seconds later she popped out of her room completely dressed and with her hair combed. She said, "Mommy, I was trying to surprise you!" Well, I was certainly surprised, and I told her that she did a great job. And then I explained to her that when Mommy calls her name, to please answer! I felt such a void when she did not answer me right away.

I wonder if that is the way God feels when we wake up and He is calling our name to tell us good morning and we do not answer Him? Say "good morning" to your Father; spend precious time with Him. And remember, He's the one who gave you this day.

Set the time of day and a time frame. In other words, make an appointment with God!

Please read 1 Samuel 1:19; 2 Chronicles 29:20; Job 1:5; and Mark 1:35.

What do these scriptures have in common?

_____

Hannah, King Hezekiah, Job, and Jesus all arose in the morning and spent time with God.

Now read Psalm 5:3. Fill in the blanks.

In the morning, O Lord, _____;
In the morning_____ and
wait in _____.

How beautiful these words are. Take a moment, shut your eyes and say this scripture to yourself. Let God's Words penetrate your heart!

Setting the time of day and a time frame is very crucial. My pastor stated this very clearly one morning when he said that we need to give God all we have first thing in the morning, not what is left at the end of the day. Making Bible study and prayer time a priority in your life will be the difference in whether you have joy and satisfaction or not. When you are obedient to God, He will bring balance into your life. Obedience **is** the key!

Please read Jeremiah 29:11-14.

What does the Lord do when we pray?

_____

He says He will listen.

<u>Melanie:</u>
Here are three simple steps to follow.

1. **Wake up earlier than usual, as much time as your schedule will allow.** For example: When you wake up at 5:00 am, the house is very quiet and there are fewer distractions. Your mind will be fresh and clear, ready to receive Him. Ask for His holy presence to shine upon you, just you and Him, creating an intimate relationship together.

2. **Set up a time frame.** For example: Divide your time between prayer and Bible study, depending on the type of study you are doing. Set a timer if you have to stay on schedule. We all lead busy lives, and this is one more area where we need to have balance.

3. **Keep a prayer journal.** List all your prayer requests. Keep adding and dating answered prayers. Try not to get overwhelmed by the number of prayer requests you have. Pray as many as you can in your allotted time. Place a pencil mark where you stopped and continue where you left off the next day. Sometimes you may have one particular prayer request that is heavy on your heart and you spend the entire time on it. That's okay! You are pouring it out to God, and that is what He wants.

What changes do I need to make?

_____

_____

What is the Lord teaching me through His Word today?

_____

_____

_____

What have I done today that has eternal value?

_____

_____

_____

Please write your Memory Scripture in the space below.

_____

_____

_____

DAY THREE

Praying

<u>**Traci:**</u>
My family and I live in a state where we have really cold weather six months out of the year. Yes, we have it all: snow, ice and sleet! Our oldest child Jake is old enough to drive, so needless to say, I PRAY A LOT!

The Bible tells us to pray without ceasing. Today we will learn more about what the Bible teaches us about prayer.

<u>**Melanie:**</u>
Psalm 63:1-3: "O God, you are my God, earnestly I seek you; my soul thirsts for you, my body longs for you, in a dry and weary land where there is no water. I have seen you in the sanctuary and beheld your power and your glory. Because your love is better than life, my lips will glorify you."

Do you earnestly seek your Father? Does your body long for Him in a dry and weary land where there is no water? Do you acknowledge His power and glory? Do your lips always glorify Him?

How did this scripture speak to your heart?

_____

_____

<u>**Traci:**</u>
The Lord's Prayer is very special to me, and I can still remember the first time I heard it. When I was pregnant with my babies, I used to sing it to them every night. It was important to me that my children know their heavenly Father from an early age, even while still in the womb.

What is the Lord teaching me through His Word today?

_____

_____

_____

What have I done today that has eternal value?

_____

_____

_____

Please write your Memory Scripture in the space below.

_____

_____

_____

DAY THREE

Praying

<u>**Traci:**</u>
My family and I live in a state where we have really cold weather six months out of the year. Yes, we have it all: snow, ice and sleet! Our oldest child Jake is old enough to drive, so needless to say, I PRAY A LOT!

The Bible tells us to pray without ceasing. Today we will learn more about what the Bible teaches us about prayer.

<u>**Melanie:**</u>
Psalm 63:1-3: "O God, you are my God, earnestly I seek you; my soul thirsts for you, my body longs for you, in a dry and weary land where there is no water. I have seen you in the sanctuary and beheld your power and your glory. Because your love is better than life, my lips will glorify you."

Do you earnestly seek your Father? Does your body long for Him in a dry and weary land where there is no water? Do you acknowledge His power and glory? Do your lips always glorify Him?

How did this scripture speak to your heart?

_____

_____

<u>**Traci:**</u>
The Lord's Prayer is very special to me, and I can still remember the first time I heard it. When I was pregnant with my babies, I used to sing it to them every night. It was important to me that my children know their heavenly Father from an early age, even while still in the womb.

Please read Matthew 6:5-15.

How does the Father tell us to pray?

_____

_____

Do you have a special place where you pray? Yes / No

Where is it?

_____

Now read Matthew 7:7-8.
Leave your Bible open to this verse; we will continue reading verses 9-12.

Fill in the blanks.
Ask_____
Seek_____
Knock_____

What are you asking, seeking, and knocking for?

_____

_____

_____

Discussion Question: Has God ever answered a long-term prayer for you? If so, explain:

_____

_____

_____

_____

_____

_____

Do you like giving your children something they really want? When your child wants something, do you immediately drop everything, run to the store, and buy it for them? Yes / No

Why or Why not?

_____

Sometimes they have to wait until the time is right. They may have to do chores to earn money for it. Or, you may want to surprise them on their birthday or Christmas. So you make them wait. Say your child wakes up and wants ice cream for breakfast. Do you immediately run to the freezer and ask him whether he wants vanilla or chocolate? Most of us would tell our children they need to eat breakfast and lunch before they can have any ice cream. Then and only then, if they don't whine and cry about it!

We do the same thing to our heavenly Father; we ask, seek, and knock, expecting Him to drop everything in His heavenly realm just to send our request through overnight delivery! It's not that God doesn't answer our prayers, because He does, each and every one of them! But sometimes He answers our prayer with a yes, sometimes with a no, and sometimes He says to wait. God has His own timetable. He sees your life from beginning to end, and only He knows exactly what you need and when you need it answered.

Now read Matthew 7:9-12.

What does verse 11 say?

_____

_____

Our Father loves you. He wants the very best for you. We need to realize that we may be asking God if we can have ice cream for breakfast. He may say wait until you have lunch. Be patient child of God, your Father knows best.

What is the Lord teaching me through His Word today?

_____

_____

_____

What have I done today that has eternal value?

_____

_____

_____

Use the space provided below to write your Memory Scripture.

_____

_____

DAY FOUR

Praise to Jesus

Melanie:

Psalm 63:4-8: "I will praise you as long as I live, and in your name I will lift up my hands. My soul will be satisfied as with the richest of foods; with singing lips my mouth will praise you. On my bed I remember you; I think of you through the watches of the night. Because you are my help, I sing in the shadow of your wings. My soul clings to you; your right hand upholds me."

If you need to feel the presence of God, Praise Him!

Traci:

Please read Psalm 93:1-5; 95:1-7; 99:1-5; 99:9; 100:1-4, and 150:1-6. Fill in the blanks and answer the following questions.

Psalm 93:1: "The Lord_____ He is robed in_____."

How do you worship the Lord's majesty?

_____

_____

Psalm 95:6: "Come, let us _____ down in _____, let us _____ before the Lord our _____."

Do you worship the Lord like that?

_____

_____

Psalm 99:5: " _____ the Lord our God and worship at his _____ , he is _____."

Read Psalm 100:3. Why are we to praise our Lord?

_____

Read Psalm 100:4. How are we expected to enter His gates?

_____

How does Psalm 150:1-6 tell us to praise the Lord?

_____
_____
_____

How do you picture the Lord? Be specific.

_____
_____

Discussion Question: What is your favorite hymn or praise song?

_____

Write the words of your favorite hymn or praise song to God in the space below.

_____
_____
_____
_____
_____
_____

Take as long as you need right now and spend some time praising your King.

What is the Lord teaching me through His Word today?

_____
_____
_____

What have I done today that has eternal value?

_____
_____
_____

Write your Memory Scripture for Week One from memory. Be prepared to recite it in class.

_____
_____
_____

WEEK TWO SUMMARY

- **Your relationship with almighty God must come first.**
- **Remove your obstacles.**
- **Set a routine.**
- **Praying is our conversation with our Father.**
- **Praise the Lord!**

WEEK TWO - TIPS AND IDEAS

Plan your dinner menus for two weeks to a month at a time. Think ahead while creating your menu. Are you having a dinner party later in the week, or maybe you'll need to bring a covered dish to church?

Daily cleaning – Wash dishes, wipe all counter tops and fixtures, sweep if needed. Pick up towels/clothes and put them in the hamper (make sure towels are dry). Pick up toys, books, and any other items and put them where they belong. Straighten up living areas and bedrooms, and make beds. Start a load of laundry in the morning and one at night.

Set a timer while you do chores or fold laundry, as this will help you to stay on task.

NOTES

_____

_____

_____

_____

_____

_____

_____

_____

_____

_____

_____

_____

_____

DAY FIVE

Week Two Review

You did great this week! Pray and reflect on this week's lesson, and let the Lord lead you into proper balance for your life.

What did the Lord reveal to me this week about how He views my relationship with Him?

_____
_____
_____

Looking back at Day One, how will I overcome my obstacles?

_____
_____
_____

How can placing God first in my life bring balance?

_____
_____
_____

What are my action steps for this week?

_____
_____
_____

What can I share with my class regarding the topics I learned this week?

_____
_____
_____

What did the Lord teach me through His Word this week?

_____

_____

_____

What have I done today that has eternal value?

_____

_____

_____

Review your Memory Scripture and be prepared to recite it in your next class.

Week Three – For Better or Worse

Day One - One Flesh

Day Two - Love, Love, Love

Day Three – Marriage and Intimacy

Day Four - Finance, Possessions and Stewardship

Day Five - Week Three Review

We are all in different seasons of life. You are either married, have been married, or will be some day. If you are not married at this time, do you allow Christ to be your spiritual husband?

Some of this week's lesson will be geared toward married women; however, even if you are single, widowed, or divorced you will learn from the Word of God as it is presented in the lesson. God has a lot to say about love, relationships, intimacy, and the way we spend our money. Get prayed up! Open your heart to hear what God has in store for **you** this week.

WEEK THREE MEMORY SCRIPTURE

**"A new command I give you; love one another. As I have loved you,
so you must love one another. By this all men will know that you are my disciples,
if you love one another" (John 13:34-35).**

DAY ONE

One Flesh

For some of us, our husband is the priority in our life that suffers the most. We are so busy being busy that our husband ends up being last on the list. We do his laundry and prepare his meals and clean his house, and by doing so we justify that we're making him a priority in our lives. But is this really the case? No, I'm afraid not. You are already doing these things for yourself and your children. If you think that doing the chores is making your husband a priority, maybe it's time for a "God-itude" adjustment. Years ago when I was a young house-wife, I tended to busy myself with housework thinking I was doing it for my husband. But housework is not nearly the same thing as having a relationship with your husband! Just like how our relationship with God has to be a priority, our relationship with our husband also has to be a priority. After all, we are one flesh.

Please read Genesis 2:21-24.

Write down verse 24.

_____

_____

_____

There are three very important topics that we will be learning about today: marriage vows, covenants, and submission.

Please read Ecclesiastes 5:4-7.

Write down verse 5.

_____

_____

Discussion Question: How does God feel about the vows we make according to these verses?

_____

Re-read Ecclesiastes 5:7 and fill in the blanks.

Therefore _____ in _____ of God.

What should be the attitude of your heart towards the vow you make with your husband?

_____
_____

What is the attitude of your heart towards the vow you made when you accepted Jesus as your Lord and Savior?

_____
_____

Okay Ladies, here's a tough one! It may have been a few years since we said our wedding vows but let's try to recall what they were. It's okay if you don't get them perfect; just do the best you can.

Write down the marriage vows you made before God with your husband. If you are not married, write down the vows you have heard at a wedding.

_____
_____
_____
_____
_____
_____

You may want to pull your wedding video/photos out and reminisce about that very important day. As you reminisce, think about the importance of the vow you made before God.

Reminisce about the vow you made to God when you first committed your life to Christ. Where were you? How has your commitment changed you?

_____
_____
_____
_____
_____
_____

Now read Psalm 116:14.

Write down the first part of this verse.

_____
_____

A vow is a solemn promise made before God or to God. Our marriages should be a three-way covenant before God. A covenant is a binding and solemn agreement between two or more individuals: God, husband, and wife. A three-way bond or covenant is so much stronger!

Read Jeremiah 31:31-34 and 1 Corinthians 11:25.

Now read 1 Samuel 18:1-4.

Write down verse 18:3

_____

_____

If you are single, have you made a commitment vow to God to remain pure until marriage? _____

If not, now is not too late!

If time allows you this week, go back and read 1 Samuel chapters 18, 19, and 20. It is such a beautiful story of true friendship. Jonathan and David were more than just best friends; Jonathan made a covenant with David because he loved him as himself. Remember a covenant is a binding and solemn agreement between two or more individuals. It is easier for me to think of it as a promise with another person.

Ephesians 5:21 – "Submit to one another out of reverence for Christ."

Please read Ephesians 5:22-33.

Fill in the blanks.

Verse 5:22
Wives, _____ to your _____ as to the Lord.

Verse 5:25
Husbands, _____ your _____, just as _____ loved the _____ and gave himself up for her.

Precious daughter of God, He is not telling us to lie down and be a doormat. God is trying to teach us a very valuable lesson here that we are to submit out of reverence for Christ! If we cannot learn how to submit to our earthly husband, how will we ever learn to submit to our heavenly Father?

Let me tell you, this lesson did not come easily for me. I am a strong-willed individual, and for many years I thought that every decision was best if done my way. I can remember biting my tongue on several occasions when it came to submission. God did a wonderful work in my heart. As God began teaching me to be submissive to my husband, I was the one who started to get the blessing. My husband started showing appreciation and respect for me. It was a beautiful thing!

Re-read Ephesians 5:33 and write it down.

_____

_____

God tells us that we must respect our husband.

Marriages all go through peaks and valleys along the way. God can get you through the hard times; all you need do is trust in Him with all your heart. Pray daily for your relationship with your husband.

There are times when we will get frustrated with our husbands. If you are married, it is very rare if this has not happened to you already, but it's **what we do** with our frustration that will make the difference. My friend Dee Smith gave me some very good advice: "If you are angry or frustrated with your husband, don't do the laundry, prepare his meals, or clean the house for him. Do it for the Lord instead." WOW! Do you think that gave me a "God-itude" adjustment? Pretty soon I was doing the chores with a grin on my face and a song in my heart because I wasn't doing anything for my husband, I was doing it all for the Lord!

What do you think that did for my husband? His whole attitude changed toward me. I became happy because I was doing everything for the Lord; my husband became happy because my attitude had changed. It got us through a very difficult period in our marriage.

Read Ephesians 6:7-8.

What do these verses say?

_____

_____

The advice Dee gave me was biblical, but at the time I didn't even know it, but what I did know was that ... it worked!

What is the Lord teaching me through His Word today?

_____

_____

_____

What have I done today that has eternal value?

_____
_____
_____

Please review your Memory Scripture for Week Three.

DAY TWO

Love, Love, Love

Please read Colossians 3:1-14. Answer the questions below.

Where should our hearts and minds be?

_____

What are we to put to death?

_____

What are we to rid ourselves of?

_____

_____

What are we to clothe ourselves with?

_____

_____

What part of Christ's character do we need to manifest in our relationship with our husbands?

_____

Dear friend, life is too short to be frustrated and angry with your husband for leaving his underwear on the floor. Remember what made you fall in love with him in the first place. Spend time together, go on dates, find a hobby you can enjoy together, laugh together, play together, and just have fun. Remember, you are one flesh.

Do you remember the first time you laid eyes on your husband? What were your thoughts? Where did you go on your first date? How long did it take you to know that he was "the one"?

_____
_____
_____
_____
_____
_____

How did you learn about Christ? When and where were you saved and baptized? How did you first serve Him?

_____
_____
_____
_____

Every now and then we need to reflect on those beginning times that are so dear to us. It makes me smile as I reflect on those tender, early days with my husband, as well as the beginning days in my relationship with my Lord and Savior.

Please read 1 Corinthians 13:1-13. Fill in the blanks.

Start with the end of verse 2.

Without love _____ _____ _____.

Begin at verse 4.

Love is _____, love is _____. It does not _____ it is not _____. It is not _____, it is not _____ - _____, it is not easily _____, it keeps no record of _____. Love does not delight in_____ but rejoices with the _____. It always _____, always _____, always hopes, always _____.

Love never _____.

Love never fails. God is love, and He never fails. Praise God, Hallelujah, and Amen!

What is the Lord teaching me through His Word today?

_____
_____
_____

What have I done today that has eternal value?

_____

_____

_____

Please write your Memory Scripture in the space below.

_____

_____

_____

DAY THREE

Marriage and Intimacy

Well, I was certain from the beginning of writing this Bible study that I was **not** going to cover this subject. God obviously had different plans! Sometimes He has to hit me over the head with a two-by-four (spiritually, not literally) for me to listen. There are some of you taking this study that desperately need to hear what God has to say about intimacy. One thing I do know about this subject is that you cannot have a balanced marriage without it. Single ladies, please press forward, and let me encourage you to find treasures in today's scripture reading.

Let's begin today's lesson by studying what the Bible says about sexual immorality.

Begin reading in 1 Corinthians 6:18-20.

What are we to flee from? _____

If this is an area in your life that you struggle with, take it to the Lord in prayer. Your body is not your own; you were bought with a price. Every one of us has the responsibility and the privilege to honor God with our bodies.

Please read Genesis 2:18-25.

For this reason:

_____
_____
_____

Now read 1 Corinthians 7:2-7. (We will continue in verses 8-17)

What is the role of intimacy between married couples?

_____
_____

Now read verses 8-9.

Does this concern you?

_____

_____

_____

Continue to read verses 10-17.

What is Paul saying here?

_____

_____

_____

Take time to pray for your spouse right now.

Intimacy is so important to God that He devoted a whole book in the Bible about it.

Please read Song of Songs 1:1-4.
Now read Song of Songs 7:1-13.

Why is intimacy so important to God?

_____

_____

Do you think that a celebration between husband and wife relates to God's love for His people? Yes / No. Why or Why not?

_____

_____

_____

What changes do you need to make in your relationship with your spouse?

_____

_____

_____

God created intimacy between a husband and a wife to be a beautiful gift; He wants us to enjoy each other! I think many women look at intimacy as just one more chore. How sad! If this is the way you look at intimacy, pray and ask God to change your heart, as this is not the way He intended it to be. I would also encourage you to sit down with your husband and discuss your concerns. If you are feeling overwhelmed by your chore load, you could lovingly suggest to your husband that if he could help with the dishes or tuck the kids into bed, it would free up more of your time to devote to him!

If you have the proper balance of intimacy in your marriage, it will build a bond like no other. When you have that God-given bond, little things that irritate you about your spouse will seem less important.

What is the Lord teaching me through His Word today?

_____

_____

_____

What have I done today that has eternal value?

_____

_____

_____

Please review your Memory Scripture for this week.

Pray right now for the Lord to guide you in the steps that will lead you to a proper balance in your marriage.

DAY FOUR

Finances, Possessions and Stewardship

Oh yes, buckle your seat belt; here we go … finance, money, and stewardship! Just like intimacy, money is a tough subject for most married couples. But money management, keeping a budget, and tithing are areas where most of us can seek improvement, and the subject of money is very important to God. God's Word is so rich and powerful, and He specifically addresses this topic in it. If it's important to Him, it needs to be important to us.

You may not have financial issues in your household, but please press forward during today's lesson even so. There are always new things we can learn from reading God's Word.

For the rest of us who do struggle with financial issues, let me ask you this question: Do you have too much month left at the end of your money? Let me clarify: do you run out of money before all your bills are paid? Let's see what the Scriptures teach us today.

Please read Romans 13:5-8.

Write down verse 8.

_____

_____

What kind of debt do you have? Hopefully you won't need all the space provided below to answer this question!

_____

_____

_____

Discussion Question: Do you currently have a household budget? Explain:

_____

_____

If money is tight and you do not have a household budget, let me encourage you to do something about it this week. There are many resources available to help you. Search online, look in your public library, or visit the financial planning section of your local bookstore. You might also want to consider enrolling in a class that teaches money-management and budgeting skills.

What actions will you take this week to improve your financial situation?

_____

_____

Are you prayerfully seeking God about this matter? Yes / No

If not, please stop right now and give this matter over to God. Your problem is not bigger than God! He can handle it!

Now read Matthew 6:24.

What does the end of verse 24 say?

_____

Read 1 Timothy 6:3-10.

What does verse 7 say?

_____

God gives us all the possessions we have. We in turn should be grateful by being good stewards.

Please read Ecclesiastes 5:10.

Now read Malachi 3:8-12.

How did Malachi's people rob God?

_____

How are we to test the Lord?

_____

What do 1 Chronicles 29:13-14 and Psalm 24:1 have in common?

_____

_____

God has shown me many times that I cannot out-give Him. One evening during a prayer meeting, one of my friends expressed a personal financial burden. She mentioned that they barely had enough food to eat each week. At the time I was unemployed and money was pretty tight in our household, but God gave me a burden to help my friend. The next day I went to the grocery store and spent some of our grocery money on them. I enjoyed choosing each item! Feeling that my friend might be embarrassed by this gift, I asked someone else (sworn to secrecy) to deliver the groceries. Word got back to me that they were truly blessed by this anonymous gift. Now let me share what God did for me! During the next year, four families that were very dear to us moved out of state. Each family had food they had to get rid of, pantry items, refrigerator items, frozen food and meat. All of them gave their food to us! Still, to this day, I have not had to buy peanut butter or mustard! Had I not given the gift of food, it's quite possible that I would not have seen the blessing of food that God gave back to me. We cannot out-give God!

Please notice in the above story that I did not use money I didn't have. I simply shared what I had with another. God placed this area of giving on my heart, and my part in the process was simply to be obedient. God blesses obedient hearts.

We talked about honoring God in our finances, but now let's answer these more personal questions: How do I honor my husband in our finances? Do I hide purchases? Do I over-spend? Do I give to charities that he doesn't agree with? Are there expenditures I have that are not glorifying to God or my husband?

_____
_____
_____

What about tithing?
If you and your husband are not "on the same page" about tithing, I suggest you pray about it, talk it over with your husband, and give in such a way that will honor both him and God. God knows your specific situation; He will honor you for having a right heart.

Read Hebrews 13:5.

Keep your lives free from the love of money and be content with what you have, because God has said, "Never will I leave you; never will I forsake you."

God is so good; He gives us everything we have. Let's be thankful to Him and obedient stewards of His money.

What is the Lord teaching me through His Word today?

_____
_____
_____

What have I done today that has eternal value?

_____

_____
_____

_____

WEEK THREE SUMMARY

- Love one another.
- Love never fails. God is love and He never fails.
- Intimacy will build a bond like no other.
- If you owe anyone money, repay them freely and unquestioningly.
- We brought nothing into the world, and we can take nothing out of it.

WEEK THREE - TIPS AND IDEAS

Make a date with your husband at least once a month. Remember, you can always do something inexpensive like a picnic, take a hike or a walk, or go for a nice drive to a favorite location.

Make your master bedroom a sacred retreat. Let this be your special place. Decorate your room in a décor that is pleasing to both of you. Place candles around the room and light them to create a romantic mood!

Take a few minutes to tidy up your room each day. You can do this together or you can do it for him to show him you care.

Read your Bible and pray together.

NOTES

_____
_____
_____
_____
_____
_____
_____
_____
_____
_____
_____

DAY FIVE

Week Three Review

My prayer after this week's lesson is that you have a deeper love for your husband and a closer relationship with your heavenly Father. Pray and reflect on the past four days.

What has God shown me about love, intimacy, and stewardship?

_____
_____
_____

How can this bring balance to my life?

_____
_____
_____

How did this week's lesson change the way I view my relationship with my husband and my relationship with Jesus?

_____
_____
_____

What are my action steps for this week?

_____
_____
_____

What can I share with my class regarding the topics I learned this week?

_____
_____
_____

What did the Lord teach me through His Word this week?

_____

_____

_____

What have I done today that has eternal value?

_____

_____

_____

Review your Memory Scripture and be prepared to recite it in your next class.

Week Four – Precious Children

Day One – Greatest Responsibility

Day Two – Raising Godly Children

Day Three – Our Children Need Balance

Day Four – Responsibility of a Child

Day Five – Week Four Review

One of our greatest gifts from God is also one of our greatest responsibilities. Raising godly children takes a lot of effort and hard work. I can't think of too many things more important than doing what it takes to raise godly children.

During Week Four we will concentrate on parental influence, godly discipline, how to achieve balance in the lives of our children, and their responsibilities.

One day we will answer to our heavenly Father as to how we are raised our children. Don't you want to hear, "Well done, good and faithful servant?" Our heavenly Father is the best example of a good parent.

Child-raising may not be the season of life you are currently in; however, we are all children of God. I urge you to hear what God is telling you this week through His Word.

WEEK FOUR MEMORY SCRIPTURE

**"Train a child in the way he should go, and when he is old he will not turn from it"
(Proverbs 22:6).**

DAY ONE

Greatest Responsibility

This is one of the greatest responsibilities we face in our lives — raising children. I realize not everyone taking this Bible study is raising children; however, we are all children of God. Search the Scriptures and find what He wants to reveal to you through His Word this week!

Please read Deuteronomy 6:1-25.

Moses is teaching about God's commands, decrees, and laws.

In verses 6-9, why is there such a strong emphasis on teaching this to the children?

_____

Discussion Question: What can you do as a parent to ensure your children grow up to love the Lord?

_____
_____

How important is it to you?

_____
_____

What changes do you need to make as a parent?

_____
_____

Now read Deuteronomy 5:16.

Have you honored your parents? Yes / No

Why did you answer the previous question the way you did?

_____

_____

What does God command us to do?

_____

_____

Why does He command this?

_____

_____

What is the Lord teaching me through His Word today?

_____

_____

_____

What have I done today that has eternal value?

_____

_____

_____

Review your Memory Scripture for Week Four.

DAY TWO

Raising Godly Children

Parental Influence: This is the influence we have on our children. We influence our children by our priorities, our relationship with God, our attitudes, our relationship with our husband, what we say, what we don't say, what we do and what we don't do. As parents, we have the greatest impact on our children's lives.

Please read 1 Kings 9:4.

What did the Lord tell Solomon?

_____

_____

Read 2 Chronicles 17:3-4.

Why was the Lord with Jehoshaphat?

_____

_____

_____

What does Jeremiah 9:13-14 say? (You may want to read all of chapter 9 to get the full context of the story.)

_____

_____

Why did they do this?

_____

_____

In 2 Timothy 3:1-7, what was Paul saying to Timothy?

_____

_____

After reading these verses, what is your view on the importance of setting a godly example for your children/grandchildren?

_____
_____

Occasionally when my children act hateful or have a bad attitude, I hear the Lord saying, "Traci, I'm showing you this because it's the way you are treating me!" Ouch.

Have you ever felt this way?

_____
_____

<u>Godly Discipline</u>: God is our example on how to discipline the correct way.

Please read Proverbs 29:15 and 29:17.

Now Read Hebrews 12:1-13.

Why does God want us to lovingly discipline our children?

_____
_____

How should our time be spent with our children?

_____
_____

What special memories do you have about your childhood?
    __ Family traditions
    __ Vacations
    __ Family meals
    __ Attending church together
    __ Board game night
    __ Getting help with homework
    __ Having a shoulder to cry on
    __ Having someone to rejoice with
    __ Family devotional time
    __ Holidays

List other special memories that made your childhood special.

_____
_____
_____

Discussion Question: Are you creating special childhood memories with your children? Explain:

_____

_____

_____

What is the Lord teaching me through His Word today?

_____

_____

_____

What have I done today that has eternal value?

_____

_____

_____

Please write down your Memory Scripture in the space below.

_____

_____

_____

DAY THREE

Our Children Need Balance

Our lesson today may appear to be very short at first glance, but it is very important nonetheless. The focus on today's lesson is to spend time in prayer concerning our children. If you do not have children of your own, please pray for any nieces or nephews you might have, or the children of your close friends; or, focus on your personal relationship with your heavenly Father.

Children are so precious in God's sight. The Bible makes it very clear what is important to Him. We live in a day and time when we think our children need to be in baseball, softball, football, cheerleading, soccer, hockey, piano, tap, jazz, ballet, Girl Scouts, Boy Scouts, and swimming lessons! I'm not saying these things are wrong, but what I *am* saying is that anything in excess is a sin!

Please read 1 Peter 1:13-16.

How do we need to live? _____
_____
_____

Are we teaching our kids to eat, drink, and be merry? Are we sending the message that they can have their cake and eat it too? How will this prepare them for their future independence in adult life? I'm afraid that many children these days are going to be in for a rude awakening in a few short years when they wake up and realize they've become an adult. We need to teach our kids balance. Talk with you kids to find out which extracurricular activity is most important to them. Let them pick one activity per season, and then they will have time for church activities, family night, homework, and yes, even chores.

Take some time today in prayer with your Father. Lift up each of your children to God. Do your children have proper balance in their lives? Let the Lord reveal how He views the activities your children are involved in. Be open. Write down what the Holy Spirit reveals to you.

Child's Name: _____
What did God show me today about this child?

Child's Name: _____
What did God show me today about this child?

Child's Name: _____
What did God show me today about this child?

Child's Name: _____
What did God show me today about this child?

Child's Name: _____
What did God show me today about this child?

What is the Lord teaching me through His Word today?
_____
_____

What have I done today that has eternal value?
_____
_____
_____

Please review your Memory Scripture for Week Four.

DAY FOUR

Responsibility of a Child

I have learned more about my children's lives over making a salad together with them than during any other activity. We start chopping vegetables and the conversation begins. We have a system; one of them will help me prepare dinner and the other child will clean up. They switch every night. It works for us because we have two children, but you can adjust this to the number of children in your family.

Having a chore chart has also been helpful. A sample chore chart has been provided which you can feel free to copy.

Each child has a chore chart of their own, so they know what they are responsible for each day. You can do this any way that works for you. We include attitude and homework on our chore chart because most kids seem to have trouble in these areas from time to time. Post your chore chart in a place that will be easily accessible for quick reference. We post ours on the inside of the pantry door.

Please read Proverbs 14:23.

All hard work brings a _____, but mere talk leads only to _____.

The Webster's New World Dictionary describes the word "chore" as "a small or routine task." Teaching our children to be responsible will teach them accountability, dependability, and good work ethics.

Read 2 Thessalonians 3:6-13.

Paul's second letter to the Thessalonians was written to clarify his first letter. The Thessalonian people were under the wrong impression that Jesus' second coming would be happening so soon that they needed to stop their normal daily responsibilities in order to prepare. Paul wanted them to understand that they were to be steadfast, living godly lives and continuing to work for a living.

What does 2 Thessalonians 3:6-13 teach us about responsibility?

_____

_____

We need to also remember that while we are teaching our children responsibility, we must lead by example.

Now read Ephesians 6:1-4.

What does verse 4 say?

_____

_____

Are you the parent in your home, or have your children taken control? The Bible clearly says that we are to bring them up in the training and instruction of the Lord.

Do your children currently have chores? Yes / No

If so, what are they?

_____

_____

If not, get ready for change.

What is the Lord teaching me through His Word today?

_____

_____

_____

What have I done today that has eternal value?

_____

_____

_____

Write your Memory Scripture for Week Four by memory. Be prepared to recite it in class.

_____

_____

_____

WEEK FOUR SUMMARY

- **Raising godly children is one of the greatest responsibilities we face in life.**
- **Set a godly example for your children.**
- **Children are precious in God's sight.**
- **"All hard work brings a profit, but mere talk leads only to poverty." Be the parent in your home.**

WEEK FOUR – TIPS AND IDEAS

Be here now. What does this mean? Whether you are spending time with your children, husband, with friends, or at your job, your full attention needs to be where you are at that moment in time. I call it "being here now!"

Homework. Set a designated time and place for your children to do their homework.

Make children responsible for their possessions. When your children get home from school, talk about their day. Sign any permission slips and get all materials ready for the next day – right then. For younger children, you may want to place their name above their special place within the home where they keep their backpack, books, and so on.

DAY FIVE

Week Four Review

Wow, this was a challenging week! We love our children. God loves His children. I hope this study helped you gain greater knowledge of what is needed to raise godly, balanced children.

Pray and reflect on this week's lesson.

What knowledge did I gain in this week's lesson?

_____
_____
_____

How can this bring balance into the lives of my child/children?

_____
_____
_____

What actions am I taking to set a godly example for my child/children?

_____
_____
_____

How am I teaching my child/children responsibility?

_____
_____
_____

What did the Lord teach me through His Word this week?

_____
_____
_____

What have I done today that has eternal value?

_____

_____

_____

Review your Memory Scripture and be prepared to recite it in your next class.

Week Five – Child of God

Day One – Victory in Jesus

Day Two – God-centered Goals

Day Three - How Do You Handle Stress?

Day Four – Healthy Eating and Exercise

Day Five - Week Five Review

Are you living a victorious life in Christ? Do you have joy? Have you lost the direction of God's will in your life? Does stress have an impact on your life? Are you taking good care of yourself?

I cannot stress this enough to you. YOU are important to God! If you had been the only person alive when Jesus was crucified, He would have died willingly just for you! He did not place us on this earth to then sit back and watch us be miserable. He wants us to live with victory in Jesus and have joy, taking good care of ourselves while reducing the stress in our lives.

This week is for you. If you have strayed off the path that God created you to walk on, then you cannot have balance in your life. Let me encourage you to take a good look at yourself. Dig deep into God's Word this week to find the real you. Find the person that He wants you to be.

WEEK FIVE MEMORY SCRIPTURE

"How great is the love the Father has lavished on us, that we should be called children of God! And that is what we are! The reason the world does not know us is that it did not know Him" (1 John 3:1).

DAY ONE

Victory in Jesus

One of my favorite hymns is "Victory in Jesus." Our goal today is not to focus on our own earthly desires but to have victory in Jesus, the kind of joy that only God can give, and to find out who we are in Him.

You need to make yourself one of your life priorities. Hopefully by now you have learned how to say no to those things that are not on your priority list. It might be helpful from time to time to refresh your memory of that priority list that we created in Week One. You might want to print it out and post it someplace where you can be continually reminded of the priorities in your life.

Please read 1 John 5:1-5

Write down verses 4 and 5.

_____
_____
_____
_____

I don't know how anyone can even make it through the trials of this life without the victory that we have as children of God. Sometimes this is the only thing that gets me through the really hard times.

There was a time in my life that I now look back on and refer to as my "desert experience." It lasted for about nine months, which is kind of ironic to me, because it takes nine months of pregnancy to bring a baby full term. This "desert experience" happened right in the middle of writing this Bible study! I can remember weeks going by and not having one good day, and I'm not just talking about the average day to day struggles. These things that were happening were really hard things to go through, but on top of it, I felt like God had left the building and had forgotten to tell me! Day after day I prayed, read my Bible, and listened to praise music just as I had done in the past. God simply was not answering my prayers. I felt so lonely, and

I wondered if He still loved me. The only thing that helped me was my assurance from the Bible, where it says that God will never leave me or forsake me. The two things that I knew at the time about a silencing from God were that I either had unconfessed sin, or that He was testing my faith, growing me spiritually. Many times I cried out to God, and many times I prayed with my face to the floor. Stillness and quiet were all that I heard. During the beginning of this desert experience, God brought me to the book of Hebrews.

Please read Hebrews 6:7-12.

The scripture that mentions the condition of the land really spoke to my heart, especially since I felt like I was walking through the desert. My prayer was that I would be a crop useful to those for whom it is farmed because I wanted to receive the blessings of God!

"God is not unjust; He will not forget your work and the love you have shown Him as you have helped His people and continue to help them. We want each of you to show this same diligence to the very end, in order to make your hope sure. We do not want you to become lazy, but to imitate those who through faith and patience inherit what has been promised."

God brought me to this scripture every single day of my walk through the desert. Sometimes I would read it several times during the day, reminding myself that God was not unjust.

God had never "left the building;" He was there all along. He was the one who brought me to these comforting scriptures every single day. This was definitely a growing stage in my spiritual life. Although it was very difficult to go through, I know that He will never leave me or forsake me. He will never leave or forsake you either. I'm so glad my relationship with God does not depend on "my" feelings. Praise God!

If you ever come to a "desert experience" in your life, keep doing what you know is right. Keep reading your Bible every single day, spend time in prayer, praise Him even if you don't "feel" like it, keep on serving in the area where you've been serving, and finally, search for unconfessed sin in your heart every day. Believe me, if you have unconfessed sin and you are seeking God with all your heart, He will let you know what it is. Press on each day in the direction you know is right. God will let you know when it is time to change directions.

Read 2 Chronicles 20:17.

Discussion Question: What does this scripture say?

_____

_____

_____

_____

I love that! He is saying that I will not have to fight my battle, but if I will take up my position and stand firm, then the Lord will give me deliverance. He tells me to not be afraid or discouraged.

Please read Psalm 60:11-12.

With God we will gain the victory! He will trample down our enemies! We serve a great and mighty Savior!

Now read Ephesians 6:10-18.

Our struggle is not against flesh and blood, but against:

_____

_____

What are we to put on?

_____

_____

_____

_____

_____

_____

To put on the "Armor of God" is not just a prayer – it requires action. We have to do what this scripture tells us to do daily. You would not go out to the battlefield without your sword, would you? Therefore, we must read our Bible every day and be prayed up before we enter the battlefield of daily life.

Read Nehemiah 8:10.

What is the joy of the Lord?

_____

_____

Now read Psalm 84:11.

He does not withhold good things from:

_____

_____

Read James 1:2-4.

When we face trials and our faith is tested, we develop perseverance. Perseverance must finish its work so that we may be mature and complete, not lacking anything!

I don't know about you, but I want to be mature and complete — not lacking anything!

Please read Psalm 37:3-4 and Psalm 103:1-5.

If we delight ourselves in the Lord, then He will give us the desires of our hearts.

Turn back to Week One, Day One. What did you write on your list?

Fill in the blanks.

What are the desires of my heart?

_____

_____

What are my goals?

_____

_____

What are my dreams?

_____

_____

Please read Colossians 1:15-16.

What does the first part of verse 16 say?

_____

Now read Colossians 1:21-23. Fill in the blanks starting with verse 22.

But now He has _____ you by Christ's physical body through _____ to present you _____ in His sight without _____ and free from _____.

Precious child of God, He loves you!

Read 1 John 2:28-29, and then continue reading to chapter 3, verses 1-3.

I love verse 3:1. How great is the love that the Father has lavished on us, that we should be called children of God!
Read 1 John 4:4 and fill in the blanks.

The one who is in you is _____ than the one who is in the _____.

Now read Isaiah 43:1-5 and fill in the blanks.

Fear not, for I have redeemed you; I have summoned _____ by name; _____ are _____. When you pass through the waters, ____ will be with _____; and when you pass through the rivers, they will not _____ over _____. When you _____ through the _____, you will not be _____; the _____ will not set you _____. For I am the _____, your God, the _____ _____ of Israel, your _____.

Thank you, Jesus! This makes me want to jump up and down and shout hallelujah! It's so exciting; He has summoned us by name and tells us, "You are mine." God has spoken for our heart! We will walk through the fire and not get burned! Knowing this, my sister in Christ, is the way to live a life of victory!

Re-read verse 43:4 and fill in the blanks.

Since you are _____and _____ in my sight, and because _____ _____ _____.

Daughter of God, these are His Words to you. You are precious and honored in His sight and He loves YOU.

Honor and glory to Him!

What is the Lord teaching me through His Word today?
_____
_____
_____

What have I done today that has eternal value?
_____
_____
_____

Please review your Memory Scripture for Week Four.

DAY TWO

God-centered Goals

Making goals and having a plan for your life is a godly trait! Today we will learn about the plans God gave Noah, Moses, and Solomon. What are the plans or goals God has given you? Have you been obedient? Let's see what God has to say about His plans and how we are to obey Him.

Please read Isaiah 30:1 and Proverbs 19:21.

What does God say about making plans?

_____

_____

Now read Psalm 119:1-5.

How are we to be obedient?

_____

_____

It is wise to align your goals and plans with God's Word.

Read Genesis 6:9 and Genesis 6:22.

What kind of man was Noah?

_____

_____

God gave Noah a detailed plan to build the Ark.

What does Genesis 6:22 say?

_____

God gave Moses several detailed plans in the book of Exodus. Because of our limited time we will name a few and discuss only one. I encourage you to read them all when time allows. God gave Moses the plan to build the Ark in Exodus 25:10-22, the Table in 25:23-30, the Lamp stand in 25:31-40, the Tabernacle in chapter 26, the Altar of Burnt Offering in 27:1-8, the Courtyard in 27:9-19, Oil for the Lamp stand in 27:20-21, and many more.

Fast forward and read Exodus 40:1-33.

What does verse 16 say?

_____

_____

What does the last half of verse 33 say?

_____

_____

Please read 1 Kings 6:1-14.

What plan did God give to Solomon?

_____

_____

Fill in the blanks starting with 1 Kings 6:12.

"As for this temple you are building, if you follow my decrees, carry out my regulations and _____ all my _____ and _____ them, I will fulfill through you the promise I gave to David your father."

What does 1 Kings 6:14 say?

_____

_____

Do you see a pattern here? Noah, Moses, and Solomon obeyed the Lord, followed His commands, and finished and/or completed their work. Let that be our pattern of life — that we would obey the Lord and His commands and finish our work!

If you are unfamiliar with any of the examples we have covered, I encourage you to read the story more in-depth.

What plans or goals do you feel God has given you?

_____

_____

_____

What steps have you made toward achieving these goals?

_____

_____

Now read Proverbs 6:6-8.

"Even an ant stores its provisions in the summer and gathers its food at harvest. It is not like the sluggard who is a lazy person who refuses to work."

Read Luke 14:28-33.

In Luke 14 Jesus discusses the cost of being a disciple when He gives the examples of a builder estimating the cost of building a tower or a king evaluating his military strength.

What does the Bible say about making plans?

_____

_____

What is the Lord teaching me through His Word today?

_____

_____

_____

What have I done today that has eternal value?

_____

_____

_____

Please write down your Memory Scripture for Week Four in the space below.

_____

_____

_____

DAY THREE

How Do You Handle Stress?

How do I handle stress?

_____

_____

What is the main source of my stress?

_____

_____

Our family has had our share of stress. At the time of this writing, we have had five deaths, two torn ligaments on two different family members, one job transfer, one going through the process of advancement in a job, a good friend involved in a major snow machine accident, five bouts of stomach flu, children earning bad grades in school, and on top of all that, my husband and I both work fulltime jobs outside of the home.

Let's see what God has to say about stress and anxiety.

Please read 1 Peter 5:6-10.

What does verse 7 say? Fill in the blanks.

_____ all your _____ on Him because He _____ for you.

Now read Philippians 4:6-7.

How does God tell us to deal with our anxiety? _____

_____

_____

Read Matthew 6:25-27.

What does the first part of verse 25 say?

_____

_____

Jesus had to deal with some troubling situations; here are a few examples:

In Matthew 4:1 Jesus is tempted by the devil.
John the Baptist dies in Matthew 14:6-12.
In Matthew 14:16-21 crowds follow Him and He feeds 5,000.

Please read Mark 1:29-39.
Jesus was a very busy man. Verse 33 says, "The whole town gathered at the door!" Can you imagine how it would be if the whole town gathered at your door?

In verse 35, how did Jesus handle situations when He was sorrowful or troubled?

_____

_____

Throughout the Gospels there are many stories of how Jesus was constantly busy healing, teaching, traveling, and doing many miracles.

Read Matthew 26:36-44.

My friend, Jesus fell with His face to the ground and prayed!

Read Matthew 27:31-50.

Prayer: Oh precious Jesus, You have been through more than I can imagine. Thank You that we can take our stress and anxiety to You. You understand us like no one else can. You love and care for us enough that You died on the cross to forgive our sins. Thank You for what You have done for us to make us free. Nothing is too big for You.

What is the Lord teaching me through His Word today?

_____

_____

_____

What have I done today that has eternal value?

_____
_____
_____

Please review your Memory Scripture for Week Five.

DAY FOUR

Healthy Eating and Exercise

Shall I place a WARNING SIGN on today's lesson? This may be a "touchy" topic for some of us! We cannot begin to balance our lives without doing something very important for ourselves, which is eating a balanced diet and getting proper exercise. Open your hearts and minds to hear God's Word today.

Let's start out today by reading 1 Corinthians 6:19-20.

What is our body according to God?

_____

Is our body our own? Yes / No

Eating Healthy

Do you think that you eat a healthy diet? I'm not talking about healthy-sized portions! How about your metabolism? Has it started to s...l...o...w down?

Please read Proverbs 23:1-2 and 23:19-21.

What does the Lord say about gluttony?

_____

Now read Daniel 1:8-16.

Daniel resolved not to defile himself with the rich foods of the royal household.

What kinds of "royal foods" do I have in my diet?

_____

_____

Read Philippians 3:19-21.

Fill in the blanks.

Their destiny is _____, their god is their _____, and their glory is in their _____. Their mind is on_____ things. But our citizenship is in heaven. And we eagerly await a _____ from there, the Lord Jesus Christ, who, by the _____ that enables Him to bring _____ under His _____, will transform our lowly bodies so that they will be like His _____ body.

This scripture is powerful! We cannot let our stomach be our god. We need to bring <u>everything</u> under His control!

Here are some healthy eating ideas:

Drink 8 – 10 glasses of water a day.
Eat more dark leafy green salads.
Choose the leanest cuts of meat.
Eliminate sugar, white bread, white rice, or anything with starch.
Bake or broil your meats, and cut out fried foods.
Eat more veggies and fruit.
Look for "whole grains" on the list of ingredients.

<u>Exercise</u>: **(Note: If you are medically unable to exercise or are under a physician's care, God understands your situation.)**

Please check with your doctor before starting a regular exercise program.

Unfortunately, exercise is not taking care of your kids 24/7, nor is it shopping and doing chores all day. Yes, those tasks are better than doing absolutely nothing, but true exercise involves much more. Believe me, if you are beginning to make excuses about why you don't exercise, you can go ahead and stop. I've heard them all. I've said them all. I used to be the queen of excuses! I am not an expert on fitness, although it is in my work-history background. What I do know is that God gave us a body for housing His Spirit within, and he expects us to take care of His temple. Are you doing a good job taking care of your temple of the Holy Spirit?

If you are not exercising for at least 30 minutes to an hour 3 times a week, then you are not getting enough exercise.

Are you doing true exercise at least 3 times a week? Circle all that apply.

Walking 30 minutes 3 times a week
Swimming
Working out at the gym
Working out with free weights
Rollerblading
Playing a sport
Working out to aerobic videos
Kickboxing
Jogging

Discussion Question: What are you currently doing for exercise?

Explain:

_____

_____
_____

_____

EXERCISE: TRUE OR FALSE

_____ **It gives you more energy.**
_____ **It reduces stress.**
_____ **It replaces fat with muscle.**
_____ **Muscles help burn fat faster.**
_____ **It lowers cholesterol.**
_____ **Feeling better about yourself, you will be a better mother/wife.**

All of the above answers are true.
God created you, and you are precious in His sight. He wants you to take care of yourself!
Take a deep inward look at yourself.

Am I the person I want to be?

_____

_____

More importantly, am I the person God wants me to be?

_____

_____

What action steps do I need to start today?

_____

_____

What is the Lord teaching me through His Word today?

_____
_____
_____

What have I done today that has eternal value?

_____
_____
_____

WEEK FIVE SUMMARY

- You are important to God because He created all things, including you.
- Making plans and goals are a godly trait.
- Cast all your cares on Him because He cares for you.
- Our body is the temple of the Holy Spirit.
- We need to bring everything under His control.

WEEK FIVE - TIPS AND IDEAS

Drink one glass of water while you prepare breakfast, lunch, and dinner, and you will have had three of the eight glasses that you need for the day!

Get in three 10-minute workouts during the day if you can; do some stretching while getting ready in the morning, do some sit-ups before bedtime, etc.

Cut up all the veggies you will need for the week. Place in plastic baggies and keep in the refrigerator for lunches and snacks. Examples: carrots, celery, cucumber, red, yellow and green peppers, broccoli and cauliflower. This will also save time when you are preparing lunches!

Prepare your menus to include wheat spaghetti, brown rice, whole wheat breads and wheat tortillas! It's better for you!

NOTES

_____

_____

_____

DAY FIVE

Week Five Review

You've made it through a tough week! Hopefully you are in touch with the real you and also now have a greater knowledge of who God wants you to be.

Pray and reflect on this week's lesson.

What knowledge did I gain from this week's lesson?

_____
_____
_____

How can making myself a priority bring balance into my life?

_____
_____
_____

How am I making myself a priority? What proof do I have?

_____
_____
_____

What are my action steps for this week?

_____
_____
_____

What can I share with my class regarding the topics I learned this week?

_____
_____
_____

What did the Lord teach me through His Word this week?

_____
_____
_____

What have I done today that has eternal value?

_____
_____
_____

Review your Memory Scripture and be prepared to recite it in your next class.

Week Six – Home Sweet Home

Day One –Home

Day Two – Let's Get Organized

Day Three – Housecleaning Tips

Day Four - Weekly Meal Preparation

Day Five - Week Six Review

Home Sweet Home! What does God have to say about our home? We are created in His image. Let's strive to be more like Him in every aspect of our lives. Being in control of our chores will help us to have a balance on our lives.

This week is part Bible study/part tips and ideas! We are going to learn how to make a house a home and how to keep it clean, organized and free from clutter. From house cleaning tips and meal planning to organizing our drawers and cabinets! So put on those cleaning gloves, fill the bucket with water…let's go!

WEEK SIX MEMORY SCRIPTURE

"But as for me and my household, we will serve the Lord" (Joshua 24:15).

DAY ONE

Home

Okay, I realize that "Thou shalt be organized and keep a clean house" is not one of the Ten Commandments. Believe me, my house is not always clean — just ask my family! My house is "lived in." As a matter of fact, we have four people and two dogs living in our house. I'm not real sure why our laundry pile always looks as if we have 16 people living here! We have a name for our laundry…Mount Warren!

However, I do enjoy having a clean and organized home. It is the way I am wired. If my house is not livable on "my terms," I am miserable until "we" get it back into order. It is part of what makes me feel balanced.

This week's study is not to make you feel inadequate or guilty if your house is "lived in" or if you too have a mountain in your laundry room. The words from the Scriptures are God's words, not mine. The tips and ideas are to help you strive towards your own personal balance in this area of your life. This will be pleasing to you and to God as well.

Please read Luke 10:38-41.

Discussion Question: Are you more like Mary, Martha, or a little of both?

_____

_____

Whether you are more like Mary, Martha, or a little of both, the important thing to remember is to keep your priorities in order and to maintain proper balance in all areas of your life.

After you have had a full day of work, or being Taxi Mom, doesn't it feel good to finally get home? I'll admit it — I'm a homebody. I love a clean house, I love to cook fancy dinners, I love having guests over. My home makes me feel content, relaxed, and loved. God has made our house a home.

Please read Proverbs 24:3-4.

By wisdom a house is built, and through understanding it is established; through knowledge its rooms are filled with rare and beautiful treasures.

How important is my home to me?

_____

_____

How important is it for me to keep order in my home?

_____

_____

Read 2 Chronicles chapters 3 and 4.

God gave Solomon detailed instructions on how to build the temple and its furnishings. Have you ever thought about that before? God is very organized and pays attention to every detail. If we are made in His image, do you think He wants us to be detailed and organized? He wants us to be like Him! Isn't that exciting?

What does my home mean to me? Circle all that apply

    My home represents a place of....
    Danger
    Bitterness
    Stress
    Relaxation
    God
    Harmony
    Arguments
    Happiness
    Balance
    Love
    Sadness
    Hate

**Is the place where I live "Home Sweet Home" or_____ _____
_____? (Fill in the blanks)**

In our home, we should practice hospitality. The definition of hospitality is to welcome people into one's home, sharing one's home and food with others.

Please read Hebrews 13:1-2.

What does this verse say?

_____

_____

Now read 1 Peter 4:9.

How are we to offer hospitality to one another?

_____

My husband, children and I live in Alaska; we have quite a few visitors, which we love! Coming to visit us seems to give our friends and relatives an excuse to visit our beautiful state. One summer we had so many guests, I honestly wanted to place a "Bed and Breakfast" sign in the front yard! Don't get me wrong; I'm not complaining one bit! Having visitors makes us feel pretty special. But in the meantime, we want to make sure that our visitors feel pretty special too. Some of the ways we try to express hospitality is to have a clean home for them to stay in, fresh flowers in their room, fresh linens, a place to store their bags and hanging items, complete with a "Welcome to Alaska" sign in the guest room. Before our guests arrive, our family will plan a menu for at least two meals a day. We always try to include halibut and salmon, because we have an abundance of these two kinds of fish in our freezer and our guests love having Alaskan cuisine. We try to make it as nice if not nicer than if they were staying in a real "Bed and Breakfast." We do this for a two-fold reason: the first being out of obedience to the Lord, and the second being that we want them to come back and see us!

Read Romans 12:9-13.

Write down verse 13.

_____

_____

Discussion Question: How do you show hospitality?

_____

_____

_____

Prayer:Lord Jesus, help me to be more like You. Give me the desire to be detailed and organized like You are. Help me to reflect Your perfect image. I praise You, Father. In Jesus' name, Amen.

What is the Lord teaching me through His Word today?

_____
_____
_____

What have I done today that has eternal value?

_____
_____
_____

Please review your Memory Scripture for Week Six.

DAY TWO

Let's Get Organized

Life runs much more smoothly if you are organized. We waste so much time looking for matching socks or trying to remember where we put the car keys. My prayer is that you will take these tips and ideas to heart and make life a little easier on yourself. I have taught these ideas and have used these tips myself for over 18 years. They work! My mom and dad always said, "Try it, you'll like it!"

Please read Ecclesiastes 10:18: "If a man is lazy, the rafters sag; if his hands are idle, the house leaks."

Now read Proverbs 12:14.

What does this verse say?

_____

_____

Read 2 Corinthians 13:11.

Aim for perfection? Use the space below to finish writing this verse.

_____

_____

_____

There are many books available on organization! I have been researching this subject for many years, and I've provided here a list of some of the key points to staying organized. Some of these ideas I tore out of old magazines, and some I have learned from trial and error. One book that was helpful to me is entitled, *Unclutter Your Home: 7 Simple Steps, 700 Tips & Ideas*, written by Donna Smallin.

LET'S GET ORGANIZED!

❖ <u>Bill Organizer</u>: Get a bill organizer that has pockets for each month. You can also keep your monthly budget in this organizer.

❖ <u>Calendar</u>: Keep a master family calendar for all doctor appointments, games, practices, homework assignments, trash day, dinner dates, parties, etc. We keep our calendar on the inside of the pantry door. It's out of the way but everyone still knows where it is. Here is our family rule: if it is not marked on the calendar, you may have to miss it! I love the saying "Lack of planning on your part does not make it an emergency on my part." Pretty harsh but so true. You may find it easier to color code. Example: highlight all games in yellow and the practices in blue.

❖ <u>Cards and Gifts:</u> At the end of the month, buy all the cards and gifts you will need for the next month. This will save you countless trips to the store.

❖ <u>Chore Chart:</u> Refer back to Week Four for a sample chart you can use.

❖ <u>Closets/Drawers:</u> Clean out one closet and one drawer every month. Get drawer organizers for your junk drawers, place old film containers with lids in drawers to hold tacks, paper clips, safety pins, etc. Label each container.

❖ <u>Clothes:</u> Lay out your clothes/children's clothes the night before.

❖ <u>Clutter:</u> If you are watching a family TV show, have everyone jump up during the commercials to pick up any clutter and put it away.

❖ <u>Coats, boots, backpacks:</u> Set up a shelf and/or hooks in a designated area for these items. You'll be all set to go in the morning.

❖ <u>Errands:</u> Before you run errands, think about where you need to go. What might need to be dropped off or picked up nearby? Try to start at one end of town and work your way back home.

❖ <u>File Cabinet:</u> Make a file for each bill that you have. Also make a file for each family member, your automobiles, cancelled checks, doctors, receipts, taxes, etc. After paying bills, place the actual bill in the appropriate file, discarding the envelope.

❖ <u>Gift-wrap organizer:</u> Keep your gift-wrapping materials in a kitchen-sized garbage can or a cardboard box of about that size. Keep bows in a shoebox. Make sure you have extra tape and a pair of scissors that stay with it.

❖ <u>Homework:</u> Set a designated time and place for your children to do their homework.

❖ <u>Housework:</u> Always tidy up, make beds, clean dishes etc. before you leave to run errands or to have a family day. When you come home tired, the house will already be clean! I always tell my children that when the house is clean, we can leave.

❖ <u>Laundry:</u> Wash at least one load in the morning and one load at night.

❖ <u>Laundry (dirty laundry):</u> Place a laundry bin in each bedroom to keep dirty clothes off the floor.

❖ <u>Laundry (folding laundry):</u> Set a timer for 10 minutes. Have everyone pitch in; see how much laundry you can fold in just 10 minutes!

❖ <u>Laundry (sorting laundry):</u> Use laundry baskets to sort clothes by color.

❖ <u>Lunches (school/work):</u> Make lunches the night before.

❖ <u>Make children responsible for their possessions:</u> When your children get home from school, talk about their day. Sign any permission slips and get all materials ready for the next day – right then. For younger children, you may want to place their name above the spot where they store their backpack.

❖ <u>Meals:</u> Cook two, three, or four meals at once. Refer to Maximum Meal Planning for more information.

❖ <u>Menu:</u> Plan your menus for two weeks to a month at a time. Think ahead while creating your menu. Are you having a dinner party later in the week, or maybe you'll need to bring a covered dish to church?

❖ <u>Return Items:</u> Return items back where they belong. Ten minutes a day looking for misplaced items takes up sixty hours a year.

CLUTTER CONTROL

Our next lesson is on housecleaning tips, but first we need to tackle the clutter. Housecleaning is even more difficult if you cannot see the floor! There are numerous ways to de-clutter your home, but we will learn just the basics today.

❖ Start with 3 large boxes or laundry baskets, 3 small containers and several large trash bags.
❖ Title your large containers: keep, sell, and donate. The small containers are for small items such as pens/pencils, jewelry and money. Obviously the bags are for trash.
❖ Start in one area working your way all the way around the room placing each item in the keep, sell, donate or trash containers.

❖ Keep only the items that you currently use or wear; also, keep items such as children's art work, family photos, family heirlooms that are special to you and your family, CDs and videos or DVDs that you currently watch or listen to.

❖ Let go of the clothes and jewelry you have not worn in the last year, old dishes, exercise equipment you no longer use, books, CDs, videos, DVDs, magazines, shoes, linens, toys, stuffed animals, furniture, appliances, cooking utensils etc, etc, etc...If it is junking up your space and you aren't using it, then let it go. Let someone else be blessed with your unused items.

❖ The "Keep" pile – make sure that everything you plan on keeping has a place. Use shelving and storage bins to organize your room. Place similar items in each storage bin, label the bins, and stack them on your shelves. Frame your children's artwork and special family photos in matching frames as wall decorations, which is a great way to display them and it keeps them from being one more thing stuffed in a drawer. Store all recent CDs, videos and DVDs, books, and magazines on a shelf or appropriate storage unit. You may even want to alphabetize them for easy access. Store all seasonal clothing in storage bins that will fit underneath a bed.

❖ If you have a room in your home that is a multi-use space for a home office, guest room, or hobby area, split the room into three sections placing all office items together, the guest space items together, and all hobby items together.

❖ "For Sale" pile – you may want to have a yard sale or take your items to a consignment shop. I have done both. Recently I have been using the consignment shop in my town because it saves me time, they do all the work at selling the items, and I earn a small income from the items sold. Whether you have a yard sale or use a consignment shop, you can use the money you receive to purchase your shelving and storage bins.

❖ "Donate" pile – Donate the items that are in good condition and that someone else could benefit from. Be sure to get a receipt so you can use it as a tax deduction.

What is the Lord teaching me through His Word today?

_____

_____

_____

What have I done today that has eternal value?

_____

_____

_____

Please write down your Memory Scripture for Week Four in the space below.

_____

_____

_____

DAY THREE

Housecleaning Tips

Okay, I know this is probably not our most favorite thing to do, but most of us probably enjoy having a clean house. So, we can either hire someone to do the dreaded chore or learn a few tips to get the job done quickly and efficiently. There are many good books on this subject and I have read a ton of them through the years. Two of them that have been very helpful are "Speed Cleaning" and "Clutter Control" by Jeff Campbell and The Clean Team.

Please read Titus 3:14.

Write this scripture in the space below.

_____

_____

Sisters, we need to make sure that we are not leading unproductive lives!

Maybe a few of you are still with me if you have ruled out hiring someone. So here we go!

❖ Get a bucket or cleaning tray with a handle to store all of your cleaning supplies.

❖ In your cleaning tray, you will need glass cleaner, a multi-purpose cleaner (preferably one with disinfectant), furniture spray, toilet cleaner, bath/tile cleaner and a scrubbing brush or pad.

❖ You will also need cleaning cloths, paper towels, and rubber gloves.

❖ When you go to clean a room, take the cleaning tray with you and you'll already have most of everything you need.

❖ Start in one section of the room and work around the room until you are where you started.

❖ Set a timer so you will stay on task.

❖ You will also need a broom, a dustpan, a mop, a bucket, and a vacuum cleaner.

❖ Always clean the floor last. You can use a mop, but in smaller rooms, I prefer to clean the floor by hand.

DAILY, WEEKLY AND WHEN NEEDED:

DAILY - Clean dishes, wipe all countertops and fixtures, and sweep if needed. Pick up towels/clothes and put them in the hamper. Pick up toys, books, and any other items and put them where they belong. Straighten up living areas, bedrooms, and make beds. Put in one load of laundry in the morning and one at night.

WEEKLY – Dust, take out trash, change bed linens; clean stove; clean refrigerator exterior and interior; throw away spoiled food. Disinfect all countertops, wiping under everything that sits on the counters.

Sweep and mop or vacuum floors. Clean mirrors; clean and disinfect bathtubs, sinks, showers, and toilets. File bills to be paid, throw away junk mail, and pay bills.

WHEN NEEDED – Wipe down baseboards, clean windows inside and out. Turn mattress over and vacuum it. Check smoke detectors, filters, etc. Dust blinds and ceiling fans. Wash curtains, rugs, and shower curtains.

What is the Lord showing me today?

_____
_____
_____

What have I done today that has eternal value?

_____
_____
_____

Please review your Memory Scripture for Week Six.

DAY FOUR

Weekly Meal Preparation

Do you frequently get to the end of your day and wonder, "What's for dinner?" Most of our families are under the impression that we are to feed them on a daily basis. Don't get me wrong; it's a joy for me to prepare meals for my family. However, it can be very stressful if I have not planned ahead. Planning menus and preparing for your meals each week will free up more of your time, giving you the time you need to enjoy your life.

Please read Deuteronomy 12:7 and Deuteronomy 12:18.

Rejoice before the Lord your God in everything you put your hand to.

PREPARATION TIPS

- ❖ Grate all cheeses that you will need for the week.
- ❖ Cut extra veggies, some raw for lunches and snacks, the rest for soup or stew.
- ❖ Use leftover hot dog or hamburger buns for garlic bread
- ❖ Make tea or lemonade in advance
- ❖ Keep your ice trays full.
- ❖ Buy in bulk.
- ❖ Separate bulk items into daily portions.
- ❖ Cook two, three, or four meals at once.
- ❖ Plan weekly menus
- ❖ Write out a grocery list/gather your coupons
- ❖ Think ahead while you are planning your menu.
- ❖ Set up a time to do your grocery list when you know you'll be in a situation that requires you to wait, such as while you are waiting for your child to get out of practice.
- ❖ Keep an ongoing list of grocery items needed posted on your refrigerator door.

SAMPLE MENU

Week One

Sunday:	Meatloaf, mashed potatoes, green beans
Monday:	Chicken or beef shish kabob, green salad, on a bed of brown rice
Tuesday:	Chicken cacciatore, green salad, and wheat rolls
Wednesday:	BBQ ribs, pinto beans, grilled vegetables
Thursday:	Grilled steak, corn on cob, Caesar salad
Friday:	Traci's tortilla soup
Saturday:	Mozzarella halibut, steamed veggies, white or brown rice

Week Two

Sunday:	Sunday pot roast, peas, white or brown rice
Monday:	Turkey breast, yams, green beans, cranberry sauce
Tuesday:	Taco salad
Wednesday:	Grilled chicken, Caesar salad, broccoli
Thursday:	Beef stir fry, white or brown rice, green salad
Friday:	Homemade pizza
Saturday:	Hamburger or turkey burgers, wheat buns, tomato, lettuce, etc.

This is just a sample menu to get you started. There are variations in the menu to give you many different choices. Add your family favorites to give yourself three to four weeks of menus.

WEEKLY MEAL PREPARATION

Set aside a two-hour time frame for preparing some of the meals in advance. You may say that you don't have two hours to spare; however, if you do it right, you will free up about 5 to 10 hours during your week by cooking some meals ahead of time. As an example, we will use Saturday as the preparation day.

Saturday – Week One Meals

- ❖ Mix your meatloaf mixture for Sunday and place in a pie plate. (See recipe)
- ❖ Boil your chicken for Tuesday, and boil extra chicken for Friday's soup. Cut chicken into bite size pieces and finish making the soup for Friday.
- ❖ Peal and boil your potatoes for Sunday.
- ❖ Cut your veggies for the shish kabobs for Monday. Cut extras for salads (do not cut lettuce or fresh spinach in advance), snacks, and lunches. Place them in individual zip-lock baggies for freshness.
- ❖ Grate mozzarella cheese for Saturday and place in a zip-lock bag, or purchase a bag of pre-grated cheese.

Saturday – Week Two Meals

❖ Place roast in oven.
❖ Brown turkey or hamburger meat for the taco salad on Tuesday and the homemade pizza on Friday.
❖ Brown your beef for the stir-fry on Thursday.
❖ Make turkey or hamburger patties for Saturday.
❖ Cut the veggies that you will need for the stir-fry for Thursday and the pizza for Friday. Cut extras for salads, snacks and lunches. Place them in individual zip-lock baggies for freshness.
❖ Grate the cheese that you will need for the pizza on Friday and place in a zip lock bag.

You will place your cooked meat either in the refrigerator or freezer, depending on when you will need it.

RECIPES

<u>Meatloaf</u>
<u>Microwave for 17 minutes on high.</u>
1 ½ to 2 lbs. of turkey or hamburger meat
½ cup onion
½ cup bell pepper
1 egg
4 to 5 saltine crackers crushed
1 can of tomato sauce, 16 oz.
½ cup of ketchup

Mix all ingredients together except ketchup. Stand a microwave-safe glass in the center of your pie plate. Spread meat mixture around the glass. Spread ketchup on top of mixture. All the fat will be suctioned into the glass. Do not remove the glass.

<u>Shish kabob</u>
<u>Grill for 7 to 10 minutes on both sides or until done.</u>
4 chicken breasts cut into 1" squares
1 large onion
1 each of red, green, yellow bell pepper
1 carton of cherry tomatoes
1 carton of whole mushrooms

Alternate chicken, vegetables and mushrooms on a skewer stick, and then grill.

Chicken Cacciatore
Serve sauce over spaghetti noodles or mix together.
2 ½ pounds cooked chicken cut into bite-size pieces
1 medium onion chopped
1 jar of your favorite spaghetti sauce
½ tsp. dried basil
1 package of wheat spaghetti noodles

Boil chicken (save broth). Add the first four ingredients together. Cook on medium heat for 20 minutes. Cook noodles in remaining chicken broth, add more water if needed. Drain noodles.

BBQ Ribs
Place all ingredients in a crock pot and cook all day.
1 package of ribs
2 bottles of your favorite BBQ sauce
½ cup water

Traci's Tortilla Soup
Bring to boil then simmer for 1 hour.
3 to 4 chicken breasts boiled, then cut into bite-sized pieces (save broth)
1 29 oz. can puree tomatoes
1 can cream of mushroom soup
1 can cream of chicken soup
3 cups of chicken broth
10 tortilla chips crushed
1 T. chili powder
1 T. cumin
1 T. garlic puree
½ onion diced
½ tsp. cayenne
3 T. fresh cilantro chopped
½ cup of grated cheese

Mix all ingredients together. Add cheese and crushed tortilla chips right before serving.

Mozzarella Halibut
Bake at 375° for 30 minutes.
2lbs. halibut filet
2 cups mozzarella cheese
1 T. lemon pepper
½ lemon

Place halibut filet in a baking dish sprayed with Pam. Line the bottom of the dish with 1 cup mozzarella. Sprinkle lemon pepper on filet and place in dish. Squeeze lemon over filet. Add the remaining cheese and bake.

Sunday Pot Roast
Bake at 350° for 4 hours
4-6 lbs. chuck roast
1 package dry onion soup mix
2 cans cream of mushroom soup
3 medium potatoes (peeled and quartered)
3 carrots (peeled and quartered)
Mix all soups together. Add the remaining ingredients together. Pour soup on top and bake.

Turkey
Bake as directed on package.

1 Pre-cooked turkey breast, season to taste and bake as directed on package.

Taco Salad
Tortilla chips (enough to cover a dinner plate)
2 lbs. – ground hamburger or turkey
2 T. – taco seasoning
3 or 4 cups of lettuce, cubed
2 cups tomato, diced
2 cups cheddar cheese, grated
1 onion, diced
picante sauce to taste
Sour cream to taste

Layer plate with tortilla chips Sprinkle meat, cheese, lettuce, and tomato on top of the chips. Add the rest of the ingredients to taste. This can be eaten with your fingers!

<u>Grilled Chicken</u>
<u>Grill 10 minutes on each side or until done.</u>
Chicken breast (as many as you will need for your family)
BBQ sauce

Brush with your favorite BBQ sauce and grill.

<u>Beef Stir Fry</u>
2 lbs. round steak cut into ¼" strips
1 bell pepper cut into strips
½ tsp olive oil
½ onion cut into strips
½ cup broccoli, diced
½ cup snap peas
½ cup soy sauce
½ cup water
1 can water chestnuts, drained

Brown the meat; drain. Add oil, bell pepper, onion, broccoli, and snap peas; cook until tender. Add meat and the rest of the ingredients. Simmer for 30 minutes.

<u>Homemade Pizza</u>
<u>Bake as directed on pizza dough package.</u>
1 can pizza dough
Pizza sauce (enough to cover dough)
1 package shredded mozzarella
1 cup of cooked hamburger, sausage, or pepperoni
1 small can mushrooms
½ bell pepper
½ onion

Push pizza dough until it fills the pizza pan, spread sauce on top of dough, arrange all the toppings, and then bake.

<u>Gourmet Burgers</u>
<u>Grill 10 minutes on each side or until done.</u>
2 lbs. ground hamburger or turkey
1 package dry onion soup mix
¼ cup Worcestershire sauce
1 package of white or wheat hamburger buns

Mix meat, onion soup mix, and Worcestershire sauce together and grill until meat is no longer pink in the middle. To make hamburgers gourmet, serve with lettuce, tomato, cheese, onion, cooked bacon, guacamole, and grilled mushrooms.

Please read James 1:22-25:

Do not merely listen to the word, and so deceive yourselves. Do what it says. Anyone who listens to the word but does not do what it says is like a man who looks at his face in a mirror and, after looking at himself, goes away and immediately forgets what he looks like. But the man who looks intently into the perfect law that gives freedom, and continues to do this, not forgetting what he has heard, but doing it – he will be blessed in what he does.

Friend, do not forget the scriptures that you have learned on this journey. Do what the Bible says, and you will be blessed.

What action steps do I need to start today?

_____
_____

What is the Lord showing me today?

_____
_____
_____

What have I done today that has eternal value?

_____
_____
_____
_____
_____

WEEK SIX SUMMARY

- ❖ **"By wisdom a house is built, and through understanding it is established; through knowledge its rooms are filled with rare and beautiful treasures" (Proverbs 24:3).**
- ❖ God is very organized and pays attention to every detail.
- ❖ We need to reflect God's perfect image.
- ❖ Planning menus and preparing most of your meals in advance will free up more of your time, giving you the time you need to enjoy life.
- ❖ Rejoice before the Lord your God in all that you put your hand to!

NOTES

_____
_____
_____
_____
_____
_____
_____
_____
_____
_____
_____
_____
_____
_____
_____
_____
_____
_____
_____
_____
_____
_____

DAY FIVE

Week Six Review

It has been such a pleasure for me to share this journey with you. I pray that the weeks you have spent in God's Word have prepared you with the tools you need to live a life that is in balance with our Creator. Let me encourage you to continue to live your life making choices that have eternal value.

Please read Titus 2:3-5.

If you are an older woman, what are you to do?

_____

_____

_____

If you are a younger woman, what are you to do?

_____

_____

_____

This Bible study may be used as a mentoring tool on how to live a balanced life God's way. Pray and ask God whom you should mentor with this information.

Write the names of those that come to your mind.

_____

_____

_____

"Each one should use whatever gift he has received to serve others, faithfully administering God's grace in its various forms. If anyone speaks, he should do it as one speaking the very words of God. If anyone serves, he should do it with the strength God provides, so that in all things God may be praised through Jesus Christ. To Him be the glory and the power forever and ever. Amen" (1 Peter 4:10-11).

Some amazing, godly women have certainly blessed me in my lifetime. These women have led by example! My mother, Sharon Wiggins (who has prayed for me every day of my life), has always taught me to follow the Lord as well as how to be a good wife and mother. My maternal grandmother, Earlene LeBlanc, taught me many lessons on cooking, and she always portrayed how to love your family with grace. My paternal grandmother, Faye Wiggins, still to this day teaches me the importance of living a Christian life and raising a family to serve the Lord! My Aunt Jean has taught me how to be a Christian businesswoman and to always persevere to reach my goals in life. My Aunt Rita has taught me the gift of hospitality and how to be a good "big sister," because that is what she has been to me. My mother-in-law, Sandy Warren, is so wonderful that, if I'm half the mother-in-law that she has been to me, my future daughter-in-law will be truly blessed. She's the best! I would also like to acknowledge my two "other mothers," Catherine McCarty and Judy Wesley. Catherine has known me since I was four years old. She taught me unconditional love and true friendship. I even had my own "pretty" room at her house when I was a child! And Judy Wesley has taught me godly wisdom and how to endure life through Christ when the really hard times come your way.

Each of these women has taught me different strengths in life. It seems so unfair to write such short versions of how they have touched and helped mold my life. I could write a book about the things these women have taught me and the godly example they have led in their lives.

Discussion Question: Have you had any "Titus women" in your life? If so, what have they taught you?

_____

_____

_____

_____

_____

_____

Who do you set a godly example for? How?

_____

_____

_____

_____

_____

While writing this book, it brought me great joy to reflect on all that I have learned from the women who have impacted my life!

Discussion Question: What knowledge did I gain during this Bible study?

_____
_____
_____
_____
_____
_____

Discussion Question: What will I do with the wisdom God has given me through this?

_____
_____
_____
_____
_____
_____

Discussion Question: How will I influence my children or other women through what I have learned?

_____
_____
_____
_____
_____
_____

Discussion Question: What did the Lord teach me through His Word during this study?

_____
_____
_____
_____
_____
_____

Review your Memory Scripture and be prepared to recite it for your last class.

Thank you, my dear friends, for choosing "How to Balance Your Busy Life …God's Way." It has been a pleasure for me to share with you the gift God has given me. I truly hope that it has blessed you and your family. We cannot merely listen to the Word; we must do what it says as well! You have spent the last six weeks learning from God's Word. Be wise with what you have learned. Wisdom is what we "do" with the knowledge that God gives us. I encourage you to always evaluate your priorities and bathe in God's holy Word so you can live a life balanced with Him!

My prayer is that God will richly bless each woman who takes this Bible study and the families they represent.

"Therefore, since we are surrounded by such a great cloud of witnesses, let us throw off everything that hinders and the sin that so easily entangles, and let us run with perseverance the race marked out for us. Let us fix our eyes on Jesus, the author and perfecter of our faith, who for the joy set before Him endured the cross, scorning its shame, and sat down at the right hand of the throne of God" (Hebrews 12:1-2).

Child of God, you are now ready to run with perseverance the race that is marked out for you. Fix your eyes on Jesus, who is the author and perfecter of our faith. God Bless You!

WEEKLY MEMORY SCRIPTURE

WEEK ONE MEMORY SCRIPTURE
"But seek first the kingdom of God and His righteousness and all these things
shall be added to you" (Matthew 6:33 NKJV).

WEEK TWO MEMORY SCRIPTURE
"Love thy Lord your God with all your heart and with all your soul and with all your mind
and with all your strength" (Mark 12:30).

WEEK THREE MEMORY SCRIPTURE
"A new command I give you; Love one another. As I have loved you, so you must love one
another. By this all men will know that you are my disciples, if you love one another"
(John 13:34-35).

WEEK FOUR MEMORY SCRIPTURE
"Train a child in the way he should go, and when he is old he will not turn from it"
(Proverbs 22:6).

WEEK FIVE MEMORY SCRIPTURE
"How great is the love the Father has lavished on us, that we should be called
children of God! And that is what we are! The reason the world does not know us is
that it did not know Him" (1 John 3:1).

WEEK SIX MEMORY SCRIPTURE
"But as for me and my household, we will serve the Lord" (Joshua 24:15).

Balance Chart

Chore Chart

Name of Child _____

Monday	*Tuesday*	*Wednesday*	*Thursday*	*Friday*	*Saturday*

Bible Study Prayer Log

Name	Date	Prayer Request	Answer

BIBLE STUDY SAMPLE AGENDA

5 Minutes – <u>Welcome/Sign In</u>

5 Minutes – <u>Opening Prayer/Announcements</u>

15 Minutes (3 or 4 songs) – <u>Praise and Worship</u> – Use Christian CDs, Hymnals, or let attendees with musical talent lead in worship. The purpose of "praise and worship" is to open our hearts and prepare us to enter into God's presence.

30 Minutes – <u>Break-out Prayer Groups</u> - Each group has 4 to 5 women, with a prayer leader in each group. List prayer requests on the Prayer Logsheet and pray for each other, or have the prayer leader pray for the women in her group.

1 Hour – <u>Large Group Session</u> — Facilitator should initiate women to share what they have learned during the week, share discussion questions, Day Five sessions and recite Memory Scriptures together as a group. Try to give each woman a chance to share if she wishes to do so during this one-hour period.

10 Minutes – <u>Closing</u> — song (optional) and closing prayer.

Printed in the United States
85572LV00006B/59-72/A

9 781602 661677